YEAR OF
ZAYED

"The citizen is the real wealth of this land, and he is the most precious potential of this country."

Zayed bin Sultan Al Nahyan

United Arab Emirates
Society
in the Twenty-first Century

Issues and Challenges in a Changing World

Jamal Sanad Al-Suwaidi

HN666.A8 S8913 2018

Al-Suwaidi, Jamal Sanad.
United Arab Emirates Society in the Twenty-first Century: Issues and Challenges in a Changing World/ Jamal Sanad Al-Suwaidi.
._ 1st edition ._ Abu Dhabi : Jamal Sanad Al-Suwaidi, 2018.
202 Pages. : Color illustrations; 21 cm.
Includes bibliographical references (p. 187-201).

ISBN: 9789948397991 (paperback edition).
ISBN: 9789948398004 (hard cover edition).
ISBN: 9789948398011 (electronic edition).

1. United Arab Emirates--Social conditions.
2. Civil Society--United Arab Emirates.
3. Education--United Arab Emirates.
4. United Arab Emirates--Political conditions.
5. United Arab Emirates--Economic conditions.
6. Citizenship--United Arab Emirates.
7. Social change--United Arab Emirates.
8. United Arab Emirates--Politics and government.
9. United Arab Emirates--History.

All correspondence should be addressed to:
United Arab Emirates
P.O.Box 114898 – Abu Dhabi
E-mail: dr.jamal.sanad@gmail.com

DEDICATION

To His Highness

Sheikh Khalifa bin Zayed Al Nahyan

President of the United Arab Emirates

(may God protect him)

and to Their Highnesses

the Leaders of the UAE Federation

CONTENTS

Introduction

"Indeed, I am happy, and I feel this immense happiness because God has allowed me to see this country years ago in a certain state; today, I find it in another state—a prosperous and advanced one, both for the country and its people, and in every field. All of this is merely a gift from God Almighty with peace and support from Him to His servants, and His grace upon them, in His land."

Zayed bin Sultan Al Nahyan

I often revisit my earlier works – both the old and the new, whether they are books, studies, or articles in academic journals and newspapers – to revise, update, contemplate and review in light of new data and input. Imad ad-Din al-Isfahani (1125-1201)[1] (although there are those who attribute it to someone else),[2] is often credited with saying the phrase "I have seen that he who writes a book today will always think tomorrow that if he had changed this, it would have been better; if he had added that, it would have been better received; if he had brought this forward, it would have been improved; or if he had left this out, it would have been more beautiful."[3] I am also not one of those people who are able to detach themselves from their writing the moment it is published and in the hands of the reader. I believe that what was written in the past can still be used in the present and the future, especially if what was written in the past relates to wider issues, or issues in which change is neither rapid nor radical,

---

1 Abu Abdullah Imad ad-Din Muhammad ibn Safiy ad-Din al-Isfahani, more commonly known as Imad ad-Din al-Isfahani. For more on the life and lineage of Imad ad-Din al-Isfahani, see: Ahed Taha Ayyal Salman, "The Literature of Warfare of Imad ad-Din al-Isfahani" [in Arabic], PhD Diss., Mu'tah University, Karak (Jordan), 2011, pp. 1-21.

2 Some scholars attribute the quote to a contemporary of Al-Isfahani—Al-Asqalani. See: Ali bin Hasan Al-Abbadi, "Correcting a quote among scholars" [in Arabic], *Al Riyadh* (Riyadh), September 3, 2009.

3 Abdullah bin Ahmed Ibn Qudamah al-Maqdisi, *Rawdat al Nather fi Jannet al Manather* [in Arabic], (Riyadh: Al Roshd Library, n.d.) p. 42, http://shamela.ws/browse.php/book-12010/page-36

such as social issues, their complexities, and areas of cont-
roversy and divergence. These issues will continue as long as
human societies exist with their interactions, changes, and
transformations.

Over the past four decades, UAE society has witnessed
many changes, for reasons[1] both internal and external.
There are also expected changes in the coming decades, in
view of globalization, the communications revolution, developments in technology, artificial intelligence (AI), and the
end of the oil era, in addition to other factors and
determinants, both known and unknown. In light of this, I
return to the study *United Arab Emirates Society: A Future
Perspective*,[2] which I prepared 15 years ago, published by the
Emirates Center for Strategic Studies and Research
(ECSSR) in 2003,[3] and then reissued in 2014. In this
regard, the purpose of representing the ideas and views
contained in this book is not merely to recall them, nor to
repeat ideas previously published; rather, it involves a more
complex and multi-faceted objective.

---

1 For some features of this change, see: Abdullah Al-Awadhi, "Emirates Society
 and Social Structure Change," ECSSR website, July 2, 2007, https://bit.ly/
 2w9Z8z1

2 Jamal Sanad Al-Suwaidi, *United Arab Emirates Society: A Future Perspective* [in
 Arabic], Emirates Lectures Series, no. 71 (Abu Dhabi: Emirates Center for
 Strategic Studies and Research, 2003).

3 Ibid.

First, these ideas have been reintroduced, but within a new set of political, economic, social, security, and scientific contexts that give them new dimensions and meanings, which are perhaps different from the meanings acquired under the circumstances and variables years ago.

Second, it was pointed out that the challenges detailed in *United Arab Emirates Society: A Future Perspective*,[1] such as identity, human resource development, economic diversification, etc., still exist and have expanded, requiring further research and diligence by researchers, thinkers, and writers, as well as every entrepreneur with an idea, vision, or perspective. In fact, we may find that investigating these issues and linking them to the present and future of the country has become more critical than ever before, because it is about the sustainability of its development during a pivotal stage of its history and advancement. This indicates that these challenges are so complex that they require new approaches to deal with them, and to devise a plan to confront them. This is what I am trying to contribute throughout this book.

---

1 Jamal Sanad Al-Suwaidi, *United Arab Emirates Society: A Future Perspective* [in Arabic], Emirates Lectures Series, no. 71 (Abu Dhabi: Emirates Center for Strategic Studies and Research, 2003).

Third, I believe that the preoccupation of researchers, thinkers, and educational and scientific institutions with the swift pace of development in the region and the world, on the political, security, economic, and technological levels, may result in a decline in the attention given to social issues. In turn, this can lead to a reduction of popular awareness concerning issues of social change and its inherent challenges, as well as issues pertaining to UAE society. Therefore, I think that re-highlighting the study of *United Arab Emirates Society: A Future Perspective*[1] represents a contribution to raising awareness of these challenges and placing them at the forefront of academic studies, whether media, demographics, civil works, and others.

Fourth, *United Arab Emirates Society: A Future Perspective*[2] was published a decade and a half ago. Since this time, UAE society has witnessed great developments. The same is true in the regional and international environment. Therefore, I reintroduced the ideas of the study (or at least some of them), taking into account these new developments, with the need to add, delete, revise, or introduce new and different views, especially considering the fast pace of

---

1 Jamal Sanad Al-Suwaidi, *United Arab Emirates Society: A Future Perspective* [in Arabic], Emirates Lectures Series, no. 71 (Abu Dhabi: Emirates Center for Strategic Studies and Research, 2003).

2 Ibid.

changes in different fields in the world around us, which have left various societies no choice—either interact positively with the changes, or "perish."[1]

Fifth, despite multiple aspects pertaining to national security, I firmly believe that the social aspect is one of the most important, as well as the most sensitive and complex because it relates to the existence, cohesion, stability, and identity of a society or a nation.[2] Any nation with a society that is being disrupted will have its national security exposed to real danger.[3] Therefore, those who aim to undermine any country will first attempt to destabilize its social stability and create causes of conflict and tension within the community. This is the essence of Fourth Generation Warfare (4GW), clearly expressed in the title of a book—*You Are the Army of Your Enemy: Fourth Generation Warfare*.[4] This is a reference to the fact that this kind of war is aimed at destroying society from within,

---

1 This is what I discussed at length in an article published by *The National*. See: Jamal Sanad Al-Suwaidi, "The only option now is to adapt or perish," *The National* (Abu Dhabi), January 2, 2018.

2 For definitions of national security, see: "The Concept of National Security" [in Arabic], *Algerian Encyclopedia for Political and Strategic Studies*, February 12, 2016, https://www.politics-dz.com/threads/mfxum-almn-alutni.4123

3 For definitions of social security and its various aspects, see: "Social Security" [in Arabic], Bahraini Ministry of Interior website, www.policemc.gov.bh/reports/2007/August/15-8-2007/1.doc

4 See: Nabeel Farouk, *You Are the Army of Your Enemy: Fourth Generation Warfare* [in Arabic] (Cairo: Dar Al Nahda Egypt, 2016).

13

pushing its various factions into fighting for religious, ethnic, sectarian, or other reasons, and then turning society into an enemy unto itself.[1] There is no doubt that one of the sources of the UAE's strength and success, in realizing its great developmental achievements and maintaining its security and stability in a turbulent regional and international environment, is social cohesion and the absence of religious, sectarian, factional, and ethnic conflicts or tensions within its society. The Social Cohesion Index,[2] a biannual national Key Performance Indicator (KPI) specific to the UAE, measures through a poll of UAE nationals aged 17 and above the extent to which the members of society enjoy the principles and values associated with national identity, social solidarity, and social partnership in society. They are based on the basic principles of family cohesion, education, culture, equality, justice, security, participation, and national belonging. The UAE achieved 93.11 percent in 2015.[3]

---

1   Zeinab Hosni Izz-Al Din, "The Effect of 4GW on Arab National Security: ISIS as a Case Study," *International Politics* [in Arabic] (Cairo, August 10, 2017), http://www.siyassa.org.eg/News/15192.aspx.

2   A composite indicator, part of the UAE Vision 2021, that measures the level of social cohesion among people in the UAE based on the following themes: family cohesion, education and culture, equality, justice, security, participation, and national belonging, https://bit.ly/2MksGUv

3   "The UAE Marks World Happiness Day Today" [in Arabic], *Al-Ittihad* (Abu Dhabi), March 20, 2017.

Recognizing the fact that protecting society against threats is a prerequisite for achieving comprehensive and sustainable development, as well as to ensure national security in its comprehensive sense, the UAE leadership has taken significant steps aimed specifically at immunizing society against threats to its stability. In this regard, I refer to three such steps.

In the first step, the UAE was among the first Arab states to address the seriousness of cybercrimes. His Highness Sheikh Khalifa bin Zayed Al Nahyan, President of the UAE (may God protect him), issued a decree in Federal Law No. 2 of 2006 for combating information technology crimes,[1] which was amended by Federal Law No. 5 of 2012 on combating information technology crimes. These included several articles that take into account developments in the field of information technology, the resulting threats to society, and the rising level of tensions and strains within it, through social media.[2]

---

1 Obaid Saleh Hasan, "Policies by UAE Legislators to Combat Cybercrimes" [in Arabic], *Al Fikr Al Sherati*, vol. 24, no. 95, (Sharjah, October 2015), pp. 43-44.

2 Obaid Saleh Hasan, "Policies by UAE Legislator to Combating Cybercrimes" [in Arabic], *Al Fikr Al Sherati*, vol. 24, no. 95, (Sharjah, October 2015), pp. 44-45.

In 2016, His Highness Sheikh Khalifa bin Zayed Al Nahyan, President of the UAE (may God protect him), issued Federal Law No. 12 of 2016 amending Federal Law No. 5 of 2012 on combating information technology crimes,[1] taking into account the developments and changes taking place in the field of information technology, and the social challenges entailed, which need to be considered and looked into.

In the second step, the UAE took to safeguarding society against tension and instability with Federal Decree No. 2 of 2015, issued by His Highness Sheikh Khalifa bin Zayed Al Nahyan, President of the UAE (may God protect him). The decree criminalizes offending the Divine Entity, prophets, apostles, holy books, or houses of worship. It also prohibits discrimination against individuals or groups on the basis of religion, doctrine, caste, sect, race, color, or ethnic origin, and any action that may provoke hate speech or discrimination through the Internet, telecommunication networks, websites, industrial materials, information technology, or any other means of audiovisual and print.[2]

---

1 "The UAE President issues several federal laws," [in Arabic] *Al Bayan* (Dubai), July 21, 2016.

2 For the full text of the law, "Law on Combating Discrimination and Hatred," *Federal Legislations Series*, (Abu Dhabi: Judicial Department, 2016), https://bit.ly/2I0IyKO

This law is viewed as the "UAE's message to spread love and tolerance in the world."[1] In light of this, it was natural for the UAE to rank third in the national culture index linked to tolerance, openness, and accepting "the other" as part of the 2016 Global Competitiveness Report.[2]

Within the framework of the condemnation of hatred and discrimination in society and the creation of a stable and strong society comes the UAE's interest in the issue of tolerance and its disposition as a profound value in society. Hence, the post of Minister of State for Tolerance was established in February 2016.[3] At the time, His Highness Sheikh Mohammed bin Rashid Al Maktoum, Vice President and Prime Minister of the UAE and Ruler of Dubai (may God protect him), stated, "We cannot allow hatred in our country. We cannot accept any form of discrimination against any person who lives in it or is a citizen of it."[4]

---

1 Ahmed Morsi and Mohammad Salah, "The Law on Combating Discrimination and Hatred is the UAE's Message to Spread Love and Tolerance in the World" [in Arabic], *Al-Ittihad* (Abu Dhabi), July 22, 2015.

2 "UAE ranks 3rd globally based on the national culture index for tolerance" [in Arabic], *Al Bayan* (Dubai), June 1, 2016.

3 "Tolerance," The Official Portal of the UAE Government, https://bit.ly/2mvokyp

4 Ibid.

In June 2016, the UAE cabinet adopted the National Tolerance Programme,[1] which works under five main themes: the government's role as an incubator for tolerance; consolidating the role of family in nation building; promoting tolerance among young people and preventing them from fanaticism and extremism; enriching scientific and cultural content; and engaging in international efforts to promote tolerance and highlight the leading role of the UAE in this area.[2]

In the third step, the UAE is actively confronting terrorism, one of the most serious threats that can fragment societies and undermine their strength, cohesion, and stability. The UAE is alert to this danger and its negative effects on its society. The UAE issued Federal Law-Decree No. 1 of 2004 on combating terrorism offences during the time of the late Sheikh Zayed bin Sultan Al Nahyan (may God rest his soul in peace), followed by Federal Law No. 7 of 2013 concerning the establishment of the Hidaya International Center for Excellence in Combating Violent Extremism,[3] and Federal

---

1 "Tolerance," The Official Portal of the UAE Government, https://bit.ly/2mvokyp

2 Ibid.

3 On violent extremism, see: Speech [in Arabic] by H.E Obaid Salem Saeed Nasser Al Zaabi, Ambassador/Representative of the United Arab Emirates to the United Nations, in Geneva, at the Geneva Conference on Preventing Violent Extremism, April 8, 2016, https://bit.ly/2qoJAnX

Law No. 7 of 2014 on combating terrorism offences, which adopted a comprehensive view of terrorism and ways to confront it.[1]

It is in this context that I will focus on a number of issues and challenges relevant to Emirati society in a changing local, regional, and international environment. I will examine seven key issues. Chapter One deals with the experience of the union of the UAE and how it has affected UAE society, especially as the founding of the union was a pivotal moment in the history of UAE society, which has left a deep impact on all levels.

Chapter Two deals with UAE society in a changing regional and international environment, based on the fact that societies do not develop in a vacuum, but within a regional and international environment that may affect them negatively and positively, directly or indirectly.

Chapter Three examines the UAE's economic vision to prepare for the post-oil era, which is based primarily on knowledge and innovation; therefore, the chapter is aptly titled "Knowledge-based Economy: The Road to the Post-oil Era."

Chapter Four addresses education and its importance in building national human cadres. This is something the

---

1 For the full text of the law, "Law on Combating Terrorism Offences," *Federal Legislations Series*, (Abu Dhabi: Judicial Department, 2015), https://bit.ly/ 2ruuzSk

UAE has paid great attention to in recent years and has launched many pioneering initiatives for its development.

Chapter Five discusses national identity in light of the developments the UAE has witnessed over the past few years, including the growing dangers linked to the spread of extremist thought as well as the adverse effects of the demographic imbalance on UAE national identity.

Balanced political development and the guarantee it gives to enable political stability in the UAE is the focus of Chapter Six.

The last chapter, Chapter Seven, addresses the rapid, comprehensive, and unprecedented change that the world is witnessing across all fields, the impact it has on the UAE, the challenges it poses, and the opportunities it offers. The book ends with a conclusion in which I call for more attention to studies pertaining to UAE society in the coming years.

Finally, through re-addressing the ideas and perspectives previously introduced in the study *United Arab Emirates Society: A Future Perspective*,[1] improving them, and adding to them within a new contextual framework, I aim to generate

---

1 Jamal Sanad Al-Suwaidi, *United Arab Emirates Society: A Future Perspective* [in Arabic], Emirates Lectures Series, no. 71 (Abu Dhabi: Emirates Center for Strategic Studies and Research, 2003).

discussion, to enrich public discussion on the present and future, especially at a time when the UAE places great importance on looking toward its future, as well as the world's, and which sets plans for decades to come.[1]

I hope what I present will add to the discussion, research, and deliberation on these issues and challenges, and contribute, if only to a small extent, to building a brighter future for my dear homeland, the United Arab Emirates. I look forward to all of these becoming the stepping stone toward devising an integrated national strategy to address the challenges facing UAE society in the 21st century.

---

1 There are several examples, most notably, "UAE Centennial 2071," for details see, https://area2071.ae/

The UAE Union Experience:
How Has It Influenced UAE Society?

"The citizens of this country are associated both in concept and practice with the Union; the Union has become an inseparable part of their lives. They embody the Union because they are no longer mere spectators, but active participants in initiating, advocating, and advancing the Union process."

Zayed bin Sultan Al Nahyan

I n my 2003 study titled *United Arab Emirates Society: A Future Perspective*[1], I did not elaborate on the influence of the successful UAE Union experience on Emirati society in terms of values, orientations, ideas, and the nature of the relations between UAE citizens. This could be due to the fact that this influence had not yet been exposed to real tests that would clearly reveal its dimensions and aspects, raise questions about it, or draw attention to it, such as the challenges that have been encountered in the years following the publishing of the study until now. During this period, UAE society has witnessed great transformation, especially in the comprehensive, radical, and rapid modernization that is always accompanied by some aspects of social tension. It is the sort of phenomenon that always goes hand in hand with modernization in societies undergoing critical stages of transition.[2] The influence of the UAE Union experience has also been impacted by turbulent changes in the international and

---

1 Jamal Sanad Al-Suwaidi, *United Arab Emirates Society: A Future Perspective* [in Arabic], Emirates Lectures Series, no. 71 (Abu Dhabi: Emirates Center for Strategic Studies and Research, 2003).

2 Abdel Ghani Emad, *Sociology of Culture: Concepts and Problematics, From Modernity to Globalization* [in Arabic] (Beirut: Centre for Arab Unity Studies, 2006), p. 192. Samuel P. Huntington, *Political Order in Changing Societies* [translated into Arabic by Sumaya Flo Abboud] (Beirut: Dar Al Saqi, 1993) p. 59. Wissam Hussein Ali Al-Ethawi, *Modernization and Stability in the Iraqi Political System after 2003* [in Arabic] (Berlin: Democratic Arabic Center for Strategic, Political, and Economic Studies, 2018), p. 8.

regional arenas. The state has engaged in extraterritorial military operations in which it lost martyrs. UAE society went through this experience, which was a real test of its coherence and unity.[1] It became apparent through UAE society's handling of all these changes, transformations, and crises that the Union experience has deeply influenced UAE society and has become an essential element of its strength, resilience, cohesion, stability, and effectiveness.

In this context, I will touch on the aspects of the influence of the Union experience on UAE society from two angles: the influence of the Union on citizenship, and the influence of the Union on the creation of new values in UAE society.

First: The Influence of the Union on Citizenship

The Union experience, which had its foundations laid by the late Sheikh Zayed bin Sultan Al Nahyan (may God rest his soul in peace) on December 2, 1971, along with his brothers, the Rulers of the emirates, represented a landmark and an important turning point in the progress of UAE society. It is no exaggeration that this experience transformed the traditional UAE society into a modern one.

---

1   Maryam Butti, Ilke Denizli, and Tarik Chelali, "The Martyr and the Nation: The UAE, Turkey, and Algeria," Delma Institute, May 22, 2018, http://drafts.delma.io/en/the-martyr-and-the-nation-the-uae-turkey-and-algeria.

The Emirati people consist of original Arab tribes with deep-rooted historical customs, which have inherited the genuine values and principles that characterize Arab tribes in terms of the individual's unwavering tribal loyalty. Such loyalty to the tribe was the predominant factor prior to the inception of the Union where "every individual belongs to a tribal group and every tribe member is obliged to defend it, himself, and other members of his tribe."[1] Tribalism was the prevailing norm then.[2]

Within this context, the first and perhaps most important factor about the influence of the Union experience on UAE society was the transition of this society from tribalism to modern statehood based on citizenship. The Union formed, enhanced, and consolidated the idea of unity in the hearts of UAE citizens at a time when the area was divided into different emirates and populated by various tribes, where the individual's tribal affiliation had precedence over any other affiliation. Here appeared the greatness and genius of the late Sheikh Zayed bin Sultan Al Nahyan (may God rest his soul in peace) in creating a federal entity that transcends any other affiliation and

---

1 "Social life," Official Portal of the UAE Government, https://www.govern ment.ae/en/about-the-uae/culture/social-life

2 Mohamed Sadiq Ismail, *The UAE Experience: Reading in the Federal Experiment* [in Arabic] (Cairo: Al Arabi Publishing & Distribution 2017), pp. 56-57.

loyalty through citizenship, where all people are equal in terms of rights and obligation regardless of the emirate or tribe to which they belong.[1] This was not an easy enterprise in a society that had lived for not just hundreds, but thousands of years relying on traditional tribal values that were detached from the logic of statehood and its related concepts: above all the concept of citizenship.[2] It required tremendous effort by the late Sheikh Zayed (may God rest his soul in peace) to gather and unify the various tribes around inclusive national goals, putting forward causes to embrace, defend, and believe in unity, and then choose it over any other form of coexistence. That is what the late Sheikh Zayed (may God rest his soul in peace) meant when he said, "The union is an embodiment of the unified UAE people's desires, hopes, and aspirations to establish a free, decent society that enjoys strength and dignity; to build a promising future under the banner of justice and truth, and to be a pioneer and nucleus of a comprehensive Arab unity."[3]

---

1 Jamal Sanad Al-Suwaidi, *Events That Changed History* [in Arabic] (Abu Dhabi, 2018), pp. 185-192.

2 Rana Khaled, "Citizenship experiment in the UAE...belonging to the land" [in Arabic], *Al Bayan* (Dubai), October 13, 2007.

3 Sultan Humaid Al-Jasmi, "Zayed and Building of the Nation" [in Arabic], *Al Bayan* (Dubai), November 7, 2015.

Furthermore, the late Sheikh Zayed (may God rest his soul in peace) required plans, strategies, and work programs on the ground through the institutions of media, education, religion, culture and heritage, justice, and others[1] in order to create a solid and cohesive society based on the common ties of history, values, customs, and language. He created a society that believes in common ties that unify all members—ties nobler than any other secondary tribal, clan, or regional association. These are the ties of citizenship and belonging to one's homeland.

The events and developments that the Arab Gulf, in particular, and the Arab region, in general, witnessed in the last decade have proven that citizenship is stronger and more deep-rooted in the UAE than in many older societies and countries in the region.[2] This was particularly evident in the years after 2011, when the entire region faced dangerous challenges, as UAE society has shown deep belonging to the homeland, complete loyalty to the leadership, keenness to maintain the higher national interests, and unconditional

---

1 On the experience of the UAE in promoting the values of citizenship see: Abdul Rahman bin Mohammed Assiri, "Arab and International Experiences in Promoting the Values of Citizenship" [in Arabic] (paper presented at the Strengthening the Values of Citizenship and Its Role in Countering Terrorism symposium, Naif Arab University for Security Sciences, Riyadh, November 17-19, 2015) pp. 7-9, https://bit.ly/2I89wvS

2 Rana Khaled, "Citizenship experiment in the UAE...belonging to the land" [in Arabic], *Al Bayan* (Dubai), October 13, 2007.

belief in citizenship. Other countries, established long before the inception of the UAE, suffered social disintegration and fell back to sub-state, ethnic, sectarian, and religious affiliations at the expense of overall national belonging based on citizenship.[1]

Undoubtedly, the efforts exerted to reinforce awareness of history, heritage, language, and shared values and customs have largely contributed to strengthening the concept of citizenship within Emirati society. Federal institutions also played an important role in bringing together and integrating the UAE's sons and daughters in one melting pot. The UAE Armed Forces is among the top institutions that greatly contributed to the formation, promotion, and strengthening of this concept. The UAE Armed Forces' troops, who come from all emirates and tribes, stand side by side to defend their homeland, sacrificing blood and soul to protect it and to preserve its achievements. His Highness Sheikh Khalifa bin Zayed Al Nahyan, President of the UAE (may God protect him), confirmed this in his speech at the inauguration of the first military college in the UAE in 1972 (His Highness was then Crown Prince of Abu Dhabi) when he stated that the college's cadets stand side by side as a symbol for a strong

---

1 Abdul Kader Nanaa, "The Role of the Federal System in Promoting Citizenship: The UAE as a Model" [in Arabic], Al Mezmaah Studies and Research Center, https://bit.ly/2I4KMbR

and solid Union.[1] His Highness Sheikh Mohamed bin Zayed Al Nahyan, Crown Prince of Abu Dhabi and Deputy Supreme Commander of the UAE Armed Forces (may God protect him), expressed the same thought in his speech commemorating the 38th anniversary of the unification of the UAE Armed Forces by saying, "The historic decision of the unification of the Armed Forces under one command and one flag, set a solid foundation for the concept of the Union that had been instilled in the minds and hearts of Emiratis."[2]

In this context, it is worthwhile highlighting the various steps and programs that the UAE has undertaken to enhance the values of citizenship in society, the most important of which are:

1. **Watani Program:** This program, launched in 2005, aims to promote national belonging and sound citizenship practices by instilling the concepts and principles that support national identity, enhancing the policy of openness and coexistence, and introducing customs and traditions by encouraging the preservation of cultural heritage and adherence to religious tolerance and social

---

1 *Documents of the United Arab Emirates* [in Arabic] (Abu Dhabi: Centre for Documentation and Research, 1972), p. 103.

2 "Speech of Mohamed bin Zayed on the 38th Anniversary of UAE Armed Forces Unification" [in Arabic], *Al-Ittihad* (Abu Dhabi), May 5, 2014.

integration. Furthermore, by activating the youth's energy and investing it in national development, the program seeks to promote a culture of volunteering and thereby encourage Emirati youth to actively participate in voluntary work.[1]

2. **The Emirati Citizen's Code of Values and Conduct:** Approved by the UAE Cabinet in 2013, the code focuses on ways and mechanisms to cultivate a positive-thinking Emirati generation, which is aware of its responsibilities and duties toward nation, family, and community.[2]

3. **Taking into account the evolving concept of citizenship:** Citizenship is no longer just limited to national identity and belonging to the homeland. This concept has developed toward universality in the 21st century. The concept of citizenship in the 21st century is defined by the following elements: recognition of the existence of different cultures, respect for the rights and freedom of others, acknowledging other faiths, understanding and activating different political ideologies, understanding the world economy, promoting interest in international

---

1 Watani Al Emarat Foundation [in Arabic] website, http://watani-alemarat. ae/about.php

2 "Document" [in Arabic], https://www.wrd.abudhabi.ae/Uploads/Banners/111_ pdf.pdf

affairs, promotion of international peace, and participation in non-violent conflict management.[1]

The UAE took these developments into consideration in its programs to promote positive citizenship. A quick examination of the objectives of the Watani Al Emarat Foundation[2] clearly confirms this concept. Among others, these objectives aim to promote an optimal policy of openness and coexistence among all nationalities and ethnicities, and to encourage openness to other cultures, as well as religious tolerance, and social integration.[3] In this respect, we may learn from the legacy of the late Sheikh Zayed bin Sultan Al Nahyan (may God rest his soul in peace). When some Emiratis complained about high fuel prices in 1980, he ordered a reduction of fuel prices for Emiratis and expatriates alike—his directives were not just limited to Emiratis.[4] Furthermore, the UAE's policy of promoting citizenship did not focus only on the emotional aspects, it instead worked to establish a citizenship based

---

1   Rana Khaled, "Citizenship experiment in the UAE...belonging to the land" [in Arabic], *Al Bayan* (Dubai), October 13, 2007.

2   Watani Al Emarat Foundation. http://watani-alemarat.ae

3   Ibid.

4   *Zayed's Dairies* [in Arabic] (Abu Dhabi: Centre for Documentation and Research, 2003), pp. 92-93.

on social solidarity, promotion of national identity, and commitment and responsibility toward the homeland by working and exerting efforts to advance and defend the homeland and protect its achievements.[1]

4. **Leadership sets an example as a role model:** At the time when the UAE leadership worked to promote the values of citizenship through a set of different constitutional, legal, and institutional frameworks, it also set an example for the entire society through its firm belief in the values of citizenship embodied in deeds before words. The participation of the UAE sheikhs alongside their brothers in the Armed Forces on the frontlines in Yemen under one banner, defending the same common values, interests, and goals, is a clear example in this regard.

His Highness Sheikh Mohamed bin Zayed Al Nahyan, Crown Prince of Abu Dhabi and Deputy Supreme Commander of the UAE Armed Forces (may God protect him), expressed this concept clearly when he said to one of the injured servicemen during his visit to the hospital, "Theyab is not better than you,"[2] referring to his son

---

1 Rana Khaled, "Citizenship experiment in the UAE...belonging to the land" [in Arabic], *Al Bayan* (Dubai), October 13, 2007.

2 Sami Al Riyami, "Theyab is not better than you" [in Arabic], *Emarat Alyoum* (Dubai), October 12, 2015.

Sheikh Theyab bin Mohamed Al Nahyan, who was serving with the Emirati contingent in Aden. This phrase clearly shows that the UAE leadership views all citizens, including the sons of the sheikhs, as equal citizens with no privilege in terms of rights and obligations. They are alike in defending the homeland and bearing responsibility, no matter how great it might be. Sheikh Zayed bin Hamdan bin Zayed Al Nahyan and Sheikh Ahmed bin Saud bin Saqr Al Qasimi set a prominent example for the deep-rooted citizenship in UAE society, as they were injured on the frontlines in Yemen.[1] The sheikhs, like the rest of the UAE's sons, joined the National Service and Reserves and expressed their pride in taking part in this sacred national duty.[2]

Second: The Union and Creation of New Values in UAE Society

The Union established new values in UAE society that had not existed before, or were not as apparent as they became after the Union. The most important of these values are:

---

1 Mohammed Al-Hammadi, "Zayed bin Hamdan… return of a hero" [in Arabic], *Al-Ittihad* (Abu Dhabi), February, 2018. See also: "Ruler of Sharjah visits Ruler of RAK to assure on health of his son Ahmed and others" [in Arabic], Emirates News Agency, December 3, 2015, http://wam.ae/ar/details/1395288809017.

2 "RAK Crown Prince: National service is a medal of honor for the UAE citizens and a sacred national duty," *Al-Ittihad* (Abu Dhabi), December 21, 2014. See also: "Ahmed bin Mohammed and National Service Recruits took the Oath," [in Arabic], *Al Bayan* (Dubai), May 5, 2016.

35

1. **National solidarity in the face of challenges:** This was solemnly represented in dealing with the martyrs' families and relatives, as all Emirati citizens from across all the emirates have shown, without exception, their support of them. UAE society has become one unit or body—as our Prophet Mohammad (peace be upon him) said, "…like one body. When one of the limbs suffers, the whole body responds to it with wakefulness and fever."[1]

The UAE Armed Forces' participation in the operation to restore legitimacy in the brotherly state of Yemen since March 2015 has clearly revealed how strong and deep-rooted the values of citizenship in UAE society are. The UAE sons from across all emirates have fought side by side defending the homeland. Despite the shock caused by the death of a number of our soldiers, who fell as martyrs on the battlefield, this has only strengthened UAE society in its allegiance to the national leadership and higher interests.[2] All attempts by enemies to play the card of tribalism, sectarianism, and regionalism have failed because UAE society has long discarded these issues.

---

1 Hadith, saying by Prophet Mohammad (peace be upon him), reported in *Sahih Moslim*—a collection of hadith compiled by Imam Moslim ibn al-Hajjaj al-Naysaburi.

2 Sayed Zaki, "The Martyrdom of our brave soldiers created a National Epic unifying the people around their leadership" [in Arabic], *Al Khaleej* (Sharjah), November 5, 2015.

The Emiratis supported the martyrs' families and viewed each martyr as a son of the whole UAE, which "made the martyrs' families recognize that they are not left alone to their loss and sorrow and that the entire UAE leadership and people stand by and support them, and take pride in what their sons have done for the sake of their homeland."[1] Despite the fact that those who targeted our martyrs in Yemen were actually betting on, "sowing dissent and division in UAE society or between the citizens and the leadership, they failed in their endeavor. This is because martyrdom has strengthened UAE society, consolidated the cohesion of the UAE's sons, and reinforced the ties between the leadership and the people. It proved to the whole world that the UAE is tenacious and immune to all foreign penetrations."[2]

"The visit by His Highness Sheikh Mohammed bin Rashid Al Maktoum, Vice President and Prime Minister of the UAE and Ruler of Dubai (may God protect him), and His Highness Sheikh Mohamed bin Zayed Al Nahyan, Crown Prince of Abu Dhabi and Deputy Supreme Commander of the UAE Armed Forces (may

---

1 Jamal Sanad Al-Suwaidi, "The Martyr's Day: The day of immortals at the heart of the homeland" [in Arabic] *Al-Ittihad* (Abu Dhabi), November 30, 2017.

2 Ibid.

God protect him), to the mourning tents of the martyrs in the different emirates revealed to the whole world the special ties between the leadership and the people in the UAE, and came as a true embodiment of the sense of the one Emirati family that shares in happiness and sorrow."[1] All of this has enhanced the UAE's image as an outstanding model for unity and cohesion on the homefront, embodying the motto of His Highness Sheikh Mohamed bin Zayed Al Nahyan, Crown Prince of Abu Dhabi and Deputy Supreme Commander of the UAE Armed Forces (may God protect him), that "the house is united."[2]

2. **Openness to the world, acceptance of the other, tolerance, and coexistence**: These and many other values have been consolidated thanks to the Union experience, the great renaissance it brought about at all levels, and the new values that it adopted. After the inception of the Union, the UAE welcomed millions of visitors from all over the world, who came either for work, tourism, or other reasons. This has undoubtedly consolidated such values as coexistence and acceptance of the other,

---

1 Jamal Sanad Al-Suwaidi, "The Martyr's Day: The day of immortals at the heart of the homeland" [in Arabic] *Al-Ittihad* (Abu Dhabi), November 30, 2017.

2 Jamal Sanad Al-Suwaidi, *Events That Changed History* [in Arabic] (Abu Dhabi, 2018), p. 192.

placing the UAE at the forefront in terms of tolerance.[1]
The first Founding Fathers, led by the late Sheikh
Zayed bin Sultan Al Nahyan (may God rest his soul in
peace), were advocates of tolerance and worked toward
that end. In a meeting with prominent Arab religious
scholars in 1993, the late Sheikh Zayed (may God rest
his soul in peace) said, "It is imperative that scholars
should explain to the people the true essence and great
message of Islam in a manner befitting the teachings of
the true religion, which calls for wisdom and good word
when preaching the cause of Allah, so that people will
respond and address the terrorism and killings that are
being carried out in the name of religion."[2]

Therefore, Emirati society is considered one of the most
tolerant societies in the region, and the world, in accepting
the other and respecting religious, cultural, and civilizational differences. The UAE is seen worldwide as
a unique model of coexistence and peace among different
ethnicities, races, religions, and cultures.[3]

---

1 Talib Ghloum Talib, *A Journey into the Affairs of Life* [in Arabic] (Giza: Atlas
   Publishing, 2016), p. 82.

2 "Zayed and the message of religious tolerance" [in Arabic], *Emarat Alyoum*
   (Dubai), June 23, 2016.

3 Ibid.

In this context, the UAE ranked first in the region and third in the world in the Tolerance Index of the 2016 Yearbook, issued by the International Institute for Management Development (IMD) in Switzerland. The yearbook showed that the UAE had advanced by five places in the ranking since 2015 and had overtaken many countries considered to be models of tolerance such as Canada, Netherlands, New Zealand, Singapore, and Sweden.[1]

This rise in the rankings was not a coincidence; rather, it occurred because the UAE Government adopted a vision, approach, and plan over many years to promote the value of tolerance in Emirati society. In this context, the UAE Ministry of Tolerance was established in 2016, leading the UAE to become "the only country in the world that has made tolerance an institutional entity and introduced it into the Government work system."[2] His Highness Sheikh Mohammed bin Rashid Al Maktoum, Vice President and Prime Minister of the UAE and Ruler of Dubai (may God protect him), reflected on the establishment of this ministry in an article titled "Why Ministers for Tolerance, Happiness, Youth, and the

---

1 "UAE is ranked first regionally and third globally in the Tolerance Index" [in Arabic], *Emarat Alyoum* (Dubai), November 16, 2016.

2 Jamal Sanad Al-Suwaidi, "The Ministry of Tolerance… an inspiring international model" [in Arabic], *Al-Ittihad* (Abu Dhabi), August 1, 2017.

Future?"[1] It stated, "We have learned from events in our region over the past five years that we need to study, teach, and practice tolerance and to instill it in our children, both through education and our own example. We need to put in place a legal framework, policies, and initiatives that formalize tolerance. We have learned from the hundreds of thousands of dead and millions of refugees in our region that sectarian, ideological, cultural, and religious bigotry only fuel the fires of rage."[2]

Nevertheless, the promotion of tolerance did not end with government programs and actions, as it also extended to the Emirati leadership, who are role models in this regard. Perhaps the most notable example is the 2017 directive of His Highness Sheikh Mohamed bin Zayed Al Nahyan, Crown Prince of Abu Dhabi and Deputy Supreme Commander of the UAE Armed Forces (may God protect him), to rename the Sheikh Mohamed bin Zayed Mosque in the Al Mushrif district after Mary, the Mother of Jesus.[3] As a result of these factors, for the seventh year in a row, 35% of Arab

---

1 Mohamed bin Rashid Al Maktoum, "Why Ministers for Tolerance, Happiness, Youth, and the Future?" [in Arabic], *Al Bayan* (Dubai), February 28, 2016.

2 Ibid.

3 "Renaming the Sheikh Mohammad bin Zayed Mosque in Al Mushrif district to 'Mary, the Mother of Jesus'" [in Arabic], *Al-Ittihad* (Abu Dhabi), June 15, 2017.

youth chose the UAE, amongst a list of countries that also includes Western countries, as the most attractive country for them to live in and the one they wanted their own countries to emulate. These results featured in the 10th annual Arab Youth Survey 2018, compiled by Burson-Marsteller, which covered 16 Arab countries.[1]

3. **Acceptance of women's employment and participation alongside men**: Emirati society is considered one of the most advanced Arab and Islamic societies in supporting the role of women in the development process and their contribution to it. This is thanks to the societal transition in the aftermath of the Union and the vision of the late Sheikh Zayed bin Sultan Al Nahyan (may God rest his soul in peace)[2] who placed special importance on the education of women as an essential part of society. One of his most important quotes, which reveals the nature of his view on women, is when he said, "I am on the woman's side; I always say this in order to uphold her right to work and participate in the building process of her country."[3] He also said, "I completely approve of

---

1 Survey results [in Arabic] on: http://www.arabyouthsurvey.com/ar/index.html

2 For more details on the view of the late Sheikh Zayed on women and their role in society see Mariam Al Mazrouei, *Zayed and Women's Education in Abu Dhabi* [in Arabic] (Dubai: Kuttab Publishing House, 2015).

3 "Women's Process in the UAE... an outstanding track record of achievements started by Zayed and nurtured by Khalifa" [in Arabic], Emirates News Agency, August 21, 2016, http://wam.ae/ar/details/1395298989446

women in a workplace that should correspond to a woman's nature and safeguard her respect and dignity as a mother and teacher of generations. The woman constitutes a pillar of the Emirati society because she is the daughter, the sister, and the mother who brings up the next generation. I am confident that women in our young country are aware of the importance of preserving our customs derived from the teachings of our religion as a basis for the advancement of the family, which is an integral part of the development of the entire society."[1]

Furthermore, the efforts of Her Highness Sheikha Fatima bint Mubarak, Chairwoman of the General Women's Union, Supreme Chairwoman of the Family Development Foundation, President of the Supreme Council for Motherhood and Childhood, and "Mother of the Nation,"[2] played a fundamental role in improving the status of Emirati women. This is in addition to the legal frameworks to ensure the rights of women after the inception of the Union that made them equal to men at

---

1 "Zayed empowered women to achieve their rights and assume their true role in society" [in Arabic], *Al-Ittihad* (Abu Dhabi), November 2, 2007.

2 For more details on the role of Her Highness Sheikha Fatima bint Mubarak, see Jamal Sanad Al-Suwaidi, *Eternal Imprints: Figures That Made History and Others That Changed the Future of Their Countries* (Abu Dhabi, 2016), pp. 57-63. See also: Mohamed Sadiq Ismail, *The UAE Experience: Reading in the Federal Experiment* [in Arabic] (Cairo: Al Arabi Publishing & Distribution, 2017), pp. 122-139.

the constitutional level and in law.[1] Moreover, there are the institutional frameworks that were formulated to empower women such as the UAE Gender Balance Council,[2] established in 2015 and which launched the world's first Gender Balance Guide in 2017.[3]

In this respect, it is noteworthy that prior to the foundation of the Union, Emirati women were denied many rights, in particular the right to education. They were not allowed to complete their education after they reached 12 years of age, as education was limited to religious informal classes (*katateeb*). Therefore, illiteracy was widespread among women, who had no real presence in the areas of employment or the economy. This situation began to change after the late Sheikh Zayed (may God rest his soul in peace) assumed power in Abu Dhabi in 1966. He established the first school for girls in Al Ain in 1968, which saw 275 female

---

1   Wassim Husam Al-Din Al-Ahmad, *Women's and Children's Rights in Light of the Gulf Legislation and Regulations* [in Arabic] (Riyadh: Law and Economics Library, 2015), pp. 183-188. See also: Yousef Abdul Ghaffar Al-Sharif, "Women's Rights in UAE Legislation: From a Legal and Islamic Perspective" [in Arabic], *Faselah*, https://bit.ly/2Ik0MX1

2   "Gender equality," Official Portal of the UAE Government, https://bit.ly/2C6Izu8

3   *Gender Balance Guide*, UAE Gender Balance Council, https://bit.ly/2v30Suc

students enrolling in the school,[1] and this trend spread noticeably after the inception of the Union.[2] Confirmation of this is clear by the following comparison: in the academic year 1955/56, 15 years before the Union, the number of female students in all schools across the emirates did not exceed 30 students. By the academic year 1986/87, 15 years after the Union, this number had risen drastically, with 43,036 female students in all emirates.[3]

The policy of supporting and empowering women has reflected on their status across all fields. Women now occupy 66 percent of public sector jobs and there are more than 21,000 businesswomen in the UAE. In fact, businesswomen make up 10 percent of the total Emirati private sector. At the political level, the UAE Cabinet includes nine female ministers—27 percent of all cabinet ministers, which is the highest rate in the world. Moreover, there are nine women in the Federal National Council (FNC), representing 22.5 percent of

---

1 Jayanti Maitra, *Zayed: From Challenges to Union* [in Arabic] (Abu Dhabi: Centre for Documentation and Research, 2007), p. 120.

2 Sweilem Al-Azi, *Sheikh Zayed and His Role in the Emergence and Development of the UAE* [in Arabic] (Amman: Academic Book Center, 2015), p. 161.

3 Aisha Ahmed Bashir et al., *The Family in the UAE* [in Arabic] (Sharjah: Sociologist Association, 1994), p. 116.

the total number of council members, while the council has also been chaired by a woman since November 2015. Women have also proved their presence in the diplomatic corps, judiciary, police, armed forces, and all other national fields without exception.[1]

The UAE ranked second among Arab countries in terms of achieving gender balance, according to the Global Gender Gap Report 2017.[2] Undoubtedly, Emirati women's engagement in public affairs, participation in all fields of national action without exception, and their achievements at different levels have brought about significant social transformation. These include: reinforcing the positive view of women and their role in society; their contribution to the development field; enhancing the image of Emirati society as an open society; and promoting the values of equality, citizenship, and non-discrimination on the basis of gender, race, or religion.

4. **Promoting a culture of excellence within UAE society:** Because of the Union and the great successes and

---

1 "Women," Official Portal of the UAE Government, https://bit.ly/2PpEvqE See also: "Women and Political Participation in the UAE" [in Arabic], UAE Ministry of State for the Federal National Council Affairs, https://bit.ly/2wmFd2Y

2 *The Global Gender Gap Report 2017*, World Economic Forum, http://www3.weforum.org/docs/WEF_GGGR_2017.pdf

accomplishments of the UAE, which allowed the country to rise into the ranks of developed countries at the regional and international levels, significant values have gained prominence in Emirati society. The main value is that of confidence in oneself and in one's ability to excel, advance, and occupy first place.[1] This has led to the strong engagement of the Emirati society's sons and daughters in the field of education and their entry into all fields of employment without fear or hesitation, including the field of modern technology with all its inherent difficulties and complexities.

This does not occur arbitrarily, as it is based on a leadership approach that instills this spirit in the citizens through deeds before words. In this context, His Highness Sheikh Mohammed bin Rashid Al Maktoum, Vice President and Prime Minister of the UAE and Ruler of Dubai (may God protect him), stressed that the word "impossible" was "invented by those who shun work, or those who do not want us to work." He added, "Impossible is a word used by some people to limit their ambitions, dreams, and aspirations—it is a shackle man

---

1 Mohammed Abdullah Younis, "The Emirati Model: The Philosophy, Dimensions, and Indicators of Development in the UAE" [in Arabic], *Trending Events Journal of Attitudes* v. 1, no. 5 (Abu Dhabi: Future for Advanced Research and Advanced Studies, December 2014).

places on his wrists or legs to impair his own movement. It is the biggest prison man can place himself in."[1]

Also, His Highness Sheikh Mohamed bin Zayed Al Nahyan, Crown Prince of Abu Dhabi and Deputy Supreme Commander of the UAE Armed Forces (may God protect him), said in an address to the UAE youth, "Our ambition is to compete with the world's advanced nations, such as Finland, New Zealand, South Korea, and Singapore, which have achieved success in human development, education, and the economy."[2]

The experience of the late Sheikh Zayed (may God rest his soul in peace) in building the Union state, despite all the hurdles he encountered, remains the greatest source of inspiration for Emiratis in terms of the will and determination to succeed and excel, regardless of difficulties. Since his early years, the late Sheikh Zayed (may God rest his soul in peace) dreamed of achieving unity between the various emirates, on the one hand, and elevating his country to the level of advanced countries in terms of economy, healthcare, and education, on the other. He was

---

1 Mohammed bin Rashid Al Maktoum, *Flashes of Thought: Inspired by a Dialogue at the Government Summit 2013* [in Arabic] (Dubai: Kuttab Publishing House, 2013) p. 90.

2 "Mohamed bin Zayed to the UAE Youth: You are a significant generation...we want to compete the world's nations with you" [in Arabic], *Al Bayan* (Dubai), March 9, 2017.

determined to realize his dream and turn it into reality despite all obstacles and difficulties before him. Thanks to his determination, self-confidence, and belief in his dream, he was able to transform the visions, ideas, and dreams he once drew on sand into a tangible reality on the ground.[1] The late Sheikh Zayed (may God rest his soul in peace), based on scientific visions, was keen to spread knowledge and learning. Therefore, in 1974 he initiated the first Knowledge Day in the UAE to honor distinguished students in various school stages.[2]

5. **Promoting a sense of national pride**: Success in achieving unity in the face of all challenges and risks has promoted a sense of national pride among UAE society. The UAE Union experience was able to endure, progress, and continue, while all other pan-Arab unity projects failed and collapsed. This deepened the faith of Emirati society in its uniqueness and ability to succeed, no matter what obstacles it may face.[3]

---

1 Awad Al-Arshani, *The Life of Zayed: The Knight who Conquered the Desert* [in Arabic] (Cairo: n. p., 1980) p.98. Also Wajih Abou Zekri, *Zayed from Near* [in Arabic] (Cairo: Dar Akhbar El Yom, 1991) p. 43.

2 *Zayed's Diaries, Part 1, 1966-1976* [in Arabic] (Abu Dhabi: Centre for Documentation and Research, 2003), p. 143.

3 For more details on the UAE Union experience, the obstacles it faced and how they overcame them, see: Jamal Sanad Al-Suwaidi, *Sheikh Zayed's Approach in Building the Union State* [in Arabic], Emirates Lectures Series, no. 211 (Abu Dhabi: Emirates Center for Strategic Studies and Research, 2018).

All this demonstrates that the UAE Union experience has created a new Emirati society in the truest sense of the word. This society is strong and cohesive, with its sons and daughters believing in a united homeland based on citizenship within a framework of the values of openness, coexistence, tolerance, moderation, and acceptance of others.

If we look forward to the future in light of the attempts to dismantle countries and societies in the Arab region,[1] then it is imperative to attach maximum priority to the plans and projects that aim at enhancing the values of citizenship, belonging, and faith in the unity of the UAE. This is especially important when it comes to young people and future generations, who are subject to waves of dangerous ideas and orientations that cast doubt on everything—homeland, society, religion, morals, and values.

The value of unity represents a safety mechanism for Emirati society. This has been the case since the beginning, and will remain so for the foreseeable future. This concept is expressed by the message of His Highness Sheikh Mohamed bin Zayed Al Nahyan, Crown Prince of Abu Dhabi and Deputy Supreme Commander of the UAE

---

1   "The Plans to Dismantle the Region…Would they be Executed?"[in Arabic], Al Kashif Center, May 2011, http://alkashif.org/html/center/22/3.pdf. See also: Abdul Hafeez Rahim Mahboob, *Solid Tackle: Saudi Arabia in the Face of Iranian Impulses* [in Arabic] (London: E-Kutub Ltd., 2017), p. 97.

Armed Forces (may God protect him), when, on the occasion of the 46th UAE National Day, he said, "Our unity is the source of our strength in the face of adversities; our unity is the point from which we move into building and growing our nation; our unity is the most important guarantee that we have to maintain the state of security and stability that our country has enjoyed for decades."[1]

---

1 "Sheikh Mohamed bin Zayed's UAE National Day message," *The National* (Abu Dhabi), December 1, 2017.

2

UAE Society in a Changing
International and Regional Environment

"The discoveries we constantly receive from the other side of the world should be a motivation and stimulus for us to work diligently and become one of the discoverers. We no longer want our people to remain the party that receives, consumes, and uses devices, but the one that exchanges utilities and inventions."

Zayed bin Sultan Al Nahyan

Societies do not evolve arbitrarily, but within a regional and global environment that impacts them both negatively and positively, directly or indirectly. In this context, *United Arab Emirates Society: A Future Perspective*,[1] first published in 2003, refers to numerous foreign challenges that impact the shaping of the future of UAE society, mainly globalization and the changing nature of the world order.[2]

The study indicates that the communications and internet revolution and technological advances are the major mechanisms of globalization, which is primarily demonstrated through transnational companies, the World Trade Organization (WTO), and the International Criminal Court (ICC), among others. This emphasizes that the world has become "a small village"[3] where notions such as borders and sovereignty have lost parts of their traditional meanings.[4]

Addressing the impact of globalization on UAE society, the study explores three major issues: the role of the state, national sovereignty, and identity. Regarding the

1 Jamal Sanad Al-Suwaidi, *United Arab Emirates Society: A Future Perspective* [in Arabic], Emirates Lectures Series, no. 71 (Abu Dhabi: Emirates Center for Strategic Studies and Research, 2003), pp. 6-23.

2 Ibid. p. 6

3 Hussein Ali Ibrahim Al-Falahi, *New Globalization: Dimensions and Repercussions* [in Arabic] (Amman: Dar Ghaida' Publishing and Distribution, 2014), p. 35.

4 Hasan Khalil, *Democracy, Globalization, and Wars* [in Arabic] (Beirut: Dar Al Farabi, 2010), p. 197.

role of the state, the study examines in detail this highly controversial issue from the point of view of various schools of thought, among which we list four.[1]

The first school views globalization as a new era of international economic relations. Thus, the economic role of the state, in light of globalization, is reduced, because global market forces possess the majority of the new ruling mechanisms,[2] while the economic power of the state has diminished, as new international institutions have taken over economic responsibilities.[3] Also, the ruling patterns are defined by economic interests and orientations; hence, politics has become the reflection of good economic management.[4]

The second school adopts a historical perspective that does not consider globalization a new phenomenon, rather

---

1   For more details, see: Galal Amin, "Globalization and the State," in *Arabs and Globalization: Research and Discussions of the Symposium Organized by the Arab Union Studies Center* [in Arabic] (Beirut: Arab Union Studies Center, 2000), pp. 153-170. See also: Jamal Munser, "The State in the Age of Globalization" [in Arabic], *Democracy Magazine* (Cairo, April 2, 2011), http://democracy. ahram.org.eg/UI/Front/News/129.aspx

2   Paul Hirst, Grahame Thompson, and Simon Bromley, *Globalization in Question: The International Economy and the Possibilities of Governance* (Cambridge: Polity Press, 1996). See also: Susan Strange, *The Retreat of the State: The Diffusion of Power in the World Economy* (Cambridge: Cambridge University Press, 1996), p. 3.

3   Mabrouk Rice, *Repercussions of Financial Globalization on the Banking System* [in Arabic] (Amman: Dar Al Jenan Publishing and Distribution, 2016), p. 38.

4   Jamal Sanad Al-Suwaidi, *United Arab Emirates Society: A Future Perspective* [in Arabic], Emirates Lectures Series, no. 71 (Abu Dhabi: Emirates Center for Strategic Studies and Research, 2003), p. 7.

a new stage of the evolution of international economic relations.[1] Therefore, globalization will not cause the erosion of states' authority and role in the international arena, especially as the state remains the power that preserves national culture.[2] It is hard to talk about global culture or civilization, because economic force by itself cannot promote this civilization.[3]

The third school believes that globalization is the main driving force toward the establishment of a new world order, marking a shift to reduce the state's authority.[4]

The fourth school suggests that the state will uphold its role in the context of globalization, but in line with different mechanisms, tools, and contents.[5]

In fact, this is an old-new and unresolved debate. Other factors, not only globalization, impact the role of the state, mainly the advent of some groups and forces, including

---

1 Jamal Sanad Al-Suwaidi, *United Arab Emirates Society: A Future Perspective* [in Arabic], Emirates Lectures Series, no. 71 (Abu Dhabi: Emirates Center for Strategic Studies and Research, 2003), p. 7. See also: Fred Halliday, "Globalization: good or bad?" *LSE Roundtable Discussion,* October 2000, p. 8.

2 "Jamal Sanad Al-Suwaidi: Global Changes Requires Redesigning Our Capabilities," [in Arabic], *Al-Ittihad,* (Abu Dhabi) November 18, 2006.

3 Jamal Sanad Al-Suwaidi, *United Arab Emirates Society: A Future Perspective* [in Arabic], Emirates Lectures Series, no. 71 (Abu Dhabi: Emirates Center for Strategic Studies and Research, 2003), pp. 7-8.

4 Jamal Sanad Al-Suwaidi, *Prospects for the American Age: Sovereignty and Influence in the New World Order* (Abu Dhabi, 2014), pp. 12, 25, and 68.

5 Zubeiri Ramadan, *Globalization and the State's New Job Structure* [in Arabic] (Amman: Academic Book Center, 2015), p. 5.

terrorist groups that challenge the nation state and seek its destruction.[1] Yet, what I can say in this regard is that globalization has undoubtedly affected the role of the state, as a political, economic, cultural, and security actor.[2]

Nevertheless, the state remains the principal actor that possesses the greatest ability to maintain balance and stability in societies, especially regarding economic aspects.[3] This has proven true through various critical economic junctures in history, mainly the Great Depression in the 1930s,[4] and the global economic crisis in 2007 and 2008, where the diminished role of states was one of the main causes underlying those crises.[5]

As for the impact of globalization on state sovereignty, the study stresses that globalization influences sovereignty in

---

1 Ahmad Sayyed Ahmad, "The Plight of the Arab National State" [in Arabic], *Al Ahram* (Cairo, September 20, 2017).

2 For more details, see: Jamal Sanad Al-Suwaidi, *United Arab Emirates Society: A Future Perspective* [in Arabic], Emirates Lectures Series, no. 71 (Abu Dhabi: Emirates Center for Strategic Studies and Research, 2003), pp. 6-8.

3 Ahmed Hesham Yoshae, *The Globalization of Gulf Economy: Reading into the Bahraini Experience* [in Arabic] (Beirut: Arab Institute for Studies and Publishing, 2003), pp. 44-45.

4 The Great Depression was a severe worldwide economic depression that started in the United States of America in 1929, with its negative effects impacting the entire world. It gave way to the ideas of the economist John Maynard Keynes, who called for increasing the government role in economy. See: Jamal Sanad Al-Suwaidi, *Events That Changed History* [in Arabic] (Abu Dhabi, 2018), pp. 103-112.

5 Jamal Sanad Al-Suwaidi, *Events That Changed History* [in Arabic] (Abu Dhabi, 2018), 102-103.

its traditional sense.[1] As influence has shifted from the state to international multilateral groupings, the state has fallen under further constraints, even in terms of its domestic conduct.[2] Meanwhile, the study downplays the scale of that impact, considering that the rise in multilateral efforts has not resulted in the erosion of the role of the state, since it is a key actor in international relations. Perhaps those efforts have consolidated the role of the state as a central party in multilateral agreements.[3]

In fact, the developments that took place in recent years have supported the ideas expressed in the study *United Arab Emirates Society: A Future Perspective*.[4] This can be clearly observed through two elements. The first element is the relative decline in the importance of regional and international multilateral organizations,[5] which used to be blamed for the deterioration of nation-state sovereignty. This is the case for the challenges facing the European

---

1 Jamal Sanad Al-Suwaidi, *United Arab Emirates Society: A Future Perspective* [in Arabic], Emirates Lectures Series, no. 71 (Abu Dhabi: Emirates Center for Strategic Studies and Research, 2003), pp. 15-16.

2 Ibid. p. 17.

3 Ibid. p. 17.

4 Ibid.

5 See: Abu Baker Al-Desouqi, "Regional Organizations on a Crossroad," [in Arabic], *International Politics*, October 3, 2016, http://www.siyassa.org.eg/News/11917.aspx. See also: Laheeb Abdelkhaleq, "The United Nations among the Ruins of Its Wars: An Engine Burning Itself," [in Arabic], *Al-Ittihad* (Abu Dhabi) October 24, 2016.

Union, mainly following Brexit,[1] and the regression of ASEAN,[2] as well as other organizations including the League of Arab States[3] and the GCC,[4] among others.

The second element is the emergence of a strong nationalist trend in the West, focusing on national interest and the state's role versus multilateral organizations and agreements.[5] This is represented, for instance, by the current US President Donald Trump, who withdrew from the Paris Climate Agreement on the grounds that it did not serve, from his perspective, the US national interest.[6]

---

1 Heidi Issmat Karess, "The Future of European Integration in Light of BREXIT," [in Arabic], *International Politics* website (Cairo, December 4, 2016), http://www.siyassa.org.eg/News/11914.aspx.

2 Mai Ooba, "ASEAN and Future Challenges," [in Arabic], *Al-Ittihad* (Abu Dhabi), October 18, 2017.

3 Hasan Nafea, "The Collapse of the Arab Regional System: What Next?" [in Arabic], *Al Hayat* (London), December 21, 2016.

4 Fatima Al-Sayegh, "The Gulf Crisis and the Future of the GCC," [in Arabic], *Al Bayan* (Dubai) October 22, 2017.

5 For more details, see: "The Right Wing in the West: The Rise and Effect," [in Arabic], Strategic Thought Center for Studies (Beirut), pp. 3-25, https://bit.ly/2PqB6HM. See also: Rinas Bnafi, "The Causes and Repercussions of the Rise of the Extreme Right: Analytical Study," [in Arabic], Democratic Arab Center for Strategic, Political, and Economic Studies website (Berlin, May 12, 2017), http://democraticac.de/?p=46400.

6 See: Tracy Wilkinson, "Trump's 'America first' policy changes U.S. role on global stage," *Los Angeles Times*, June 2, 2017.

Regarding the impact of globalization on national identity, *United Arab Emirates Society: A Future Perspective*[1] elaborates in detail the divergent views regarding the limits of this impact. Certain people believe it is an overwhelming and profound impact,[2] while others downplay this impact, emphasizing that national cultures have demonstrated a strong ability to face attempts to globalize culture.[3] The study asserts that there is no clear evidence suggesting that globalization has actually triggered a substantial decline in national culture, introducing the UAE and Arab Gulf states as an interesting example in this regard.[4] Some worrying manifestations of globalization's impact on national identity in these countries cannot be ignored; yet, the underlying structural factors of the Arab-Islamic combination provide the people of the region with a strong

---

1 Jamal Sanad Al-Suwaidi, *United Arab Emirates Society: A Future Perspective* [in Arabic], Emirates Lectures Series, no. 71 (Abu Dhabi: Emirates Center for Strategic Studies and Research, 2003).

2 Ayoub Dhakhlallah, *Education and Society Problems in the Age of Globalization* [in Arabic] (Beirut: Dar Al Kotub Al Illmiyah, 2015), p. 112.

3 For more details on identity and culture, see: Anthony D. Smith, "Towards a Global Culture?" in: David Held and Anthony McGrew, eds., *The Global Transformations Reader: An Introduction to the Globalization Debate* (Cambridge: Polity Press, 2000), pp. 240-242. See also: Suad Al-Araimi, UAE *Between Instilling Identity and Strengthening Belonging...An Analytical Sociological Study* [in Arabic] (Abu Dhabi: Emirates Center for Strategic Studies and Research, 2017).

4 Jamal Sanad Al-Suwaidi, *United Arab Emirates Society: A Future Perspective* [in Arabic], Emirates Lectures Series, no. 71 (Abu Dhabi: Emirates Center for Strategic Studies and Research, 2003), p. 20.

ability to adapt to the requirements of modernization while preserving their authenticity, value system, and inherited customs and traditions.[1]

Obviously, this does not mean there is not a serious underlying cultural challenge that needs to be taken into account in the UAE. First, there are extremist groups and movements, primarily the Muslim Brotherhood, which seek to shape new and distorted identities for Arab societies.[2] Second, the communications revolution has reached such excessive and dangerous levels that it has become a real threat to identity.[3] Third, in the context of the critical juncture and civilizational regression in the Arab region, certain parties seek to seize the opportunity to undermine our civilization, culture, identity, and religion, even though they are the ones to blame for this regression in Arab and Muslim societies.[4] Fourth, globalization involves the erosion of borders between countries and people; yet, it has

---

1 Jamal Sanad Al-Suwaidi, *United Arab Emirates Society: A Future Perspective* [in Arabic], Emirates Lectures Series, no. 71 (Abu Dhabi: Emirates Center for Strategic Studies and Research, 2003), p. 20.

2 Awatef Outeil Elmawaldi, "The Problem of Religious Extremism and the Cultural Identity of Society," [in Arabic], *Studies and Research Journal* no. 25 (Algiers, December 2016), pp. 71-78.

3 Reda Amin, *New Media* [in Arabic] (Cairo: Dar Al-Fajr Publishing and Distribution, 2015), p. 60.

4 Yaser Quteishat, "The Dialectic Relation between Arabs and the West: The Struggle of Ignorance and Cultural Dialog," [in Arabic], Mominoun Without Borders website, June 21, 2018, https://bit.ly/2qnbPo5

brought about cultures, thoughts, orientations, and behaviors that seriously threaten the UAE's national and
civilizational identity. I will comprehensively discuss this
issue later in a part dedicated to identity.

The second foreign challenge addressed in *United
Arab Emirates Society: A Future Perspective*[1] is the changing
nature of the world order. In this context, I discussed the
impact of the unipolar world order on the UAE's foreign
choices, shedding light on the ensuing constraints. Some
researchers claim that the world has moved beyond the
unipolar phase, and is in the transitional process toward
a multipolar world order.[2] I do not share the same opinion
for four reasons. First, the US, in terms of political,
economic, military, and cultural standards, is still the
world's foremost influential superpower, and is capable of
regulating international interactions.[3]

Second, certain global forces, primarily China, Russia,
and the European Union,[4] have recently increased their

---

1 Jamal Sanad Al-Suwaidi, *United Arab Emirates Society: A Future Perspective* [in
Arabic], Emirates Lectures Series, no. 71 (Abu Dhabi: Emirates Center for
Strategic Studies and Research, 2003), pp. 21-22.

2 Moustafa Alawai, "The Single Pole: The United States of America and
Change in the Structure of the World Order," [in Arabic], Arab Center for
Research and Studies website (Cairo), January 10, 2015, http://www.
acrseg.org/36519

3 Jamal Sanad Al-Suwaidi, *Prospects for the American Age: Sovereignty and
Influence in the New World Order* (Abu Dhabi, 2014), pp. 34-35.

4 Ibid., p. 53.

influence in the international arena; however, this is not a sign of a power imbalance at the expense of the US. Rather, it is the US that has deliberately and temporarily withdrawn from the international arena, due to specific orientations or political reasons. The US will regain its appropriate position, once the political administration in Washington is changed or adopts different approaches, as was the case following the end of the previous US President Barack Obama's term in office.

Obama's administration adopted soft power diplomacy[1] and a leading-from-behind policy, which allowed the US's adversaries and competitors to challenge its global hegemony.[2] With the arrival of Donald Trump's administration, US power has regained its predominance, as reflected in the US National Security Strategy[3] declared on December 18, 2017. The Strategy includes numerous principles that reassert US global leadership, such as the "peace through strength" principle,[4] which consists of

---

1 See: Hillary Rodham Clinton, "Leading through Civilian Power: Redefining American Diplomacy and Development," *Foreign Affairs*, October 1, 2010, https://fam.ag/ 2GPWJl9.

2 Malek Awni, "Unified Challenge: Emerging regional power and trends in the evolution of the international leadership structure," [in Arabic], *International Politics*, October 14, 2014, http://www.siyassa.org.eg/News/4937.aspx

3 "National Security Strategy of the United States of America," December 2017, https://bit.ly/2CzLLd7.

4 Ibid.

rebuilding the US military forces to maintain their dominance (the 2018 budget of the US Department of Defense reached US$700 billion); employing all available tools to protect US interests; maintaining a power balance that serves US interests in major regions worldwide; and enhancing US global influence.

Third, the major international powers, themselves, would prefer that the US remain the leader of the world order, because they seek to avoid the ensuing expenses of global leadership, while they still lack its required capacity.

Fourth, China, which some researchers refer to as a competitor to the US for global leadership,[1] does not seek to play this role, as openly expressed by several Chinese officials. Most recently Zhang Jun, the Director General of the Chinese Foreign Ministry's International Economics Department, said that "If anyone were to say China is playing a leadership role in the world, I would say it is not China rushing to the front, rather the frontrunners have stepped back, leaving the place to China."[2] Even if China wants to take over global leadership, it lacks the necessary capacity,

---

1 Tamer Ibrahim Kamel Hashem, *The Conflict between the United States of America, and the People's Republic of China and the Russian Federation as Rising Powers: A Case Study of Central Asia and the Caspian Sea* [in Arabic] (Cairo: Al Maktab Al Arabi Lil Maaref, 2014), p. 144.

2 Reuters, "Diplomat says China would assume world leadership if needed," January 23, 2017, https://www.reuters.com/article/us-china-usa-politics-idUSKBN1570ZZ.

since it does not represent an inspiring political and cultural model, as is the case with the Western model. Also, its large population is a heavy burden that limits its maneuvers in the age of globalization.[1] My book *Prospects for the American Age: Sovereignty and Influence in the New World Order* discusses this issue at great length.[2]

When *United Arab Emirates Society: A Future Perspective*[3] was first published in 2003, the regional environment was not facing as many challenges as it is today. The major challenge at that time originated from the international environment, mainly in terms of the impact of globalization; therefore, the study did not address the regional environment. However, these current challenges, primarily terrorism and extremism, seem more dangerous for the UAE and Arab societies, in light of their existential threat.[4] Terrorism and extremism have proven seriously detrimental to the security of states and stability of

---

1   Zheng Bijian, *China's Road to Peaceful Rise: Observations on its Cause, Basis, Connotation, and Prospect* (New York: Routledge; 1 edition, December 2011), p. 63.

2   For more details, see: Jamal Sanad Al-Suwaidi, *Prospects for the American Age: Sovereignty and Influence in the New World Order* (Abu Dhabi, 2014).

3   Jamal Sanad Al-Suwaidi, *United Arab Emirates Society: A Future Perspective* [in Arabic], Emirates Lectures Series, no. 71 (Abu Dhabi: Emirates Center for Strategic Studies and Research, 2003)

4   In this regard see: Jamal Sanad Al-Suwaidi, *The Mirage*, (Abu Dhabi, 2015).

societies since the 9/11 attacks carried out by Al-Qaeda on US soil.[1]

These events triggered the Global War on terrorism,[2] and demonstrated that the threat posed by terrorist groups and organizations had moved beyond local and regional borders and extended to the global scene. The attacks also revealed that any country, regardless of its capabilities, strength, and influence, is vulnerable to the evils of terrorism.[3] Islamic State of Iraq and Syria (ISIS) is an interesting example in this regard; it was first centered in Iraq and Syria, yet its danger has extended to many regions of the world, including the heart of Europe.[4]

This phenomenon has grown in the Arab region and beyond, reaching its peak following the upheavals that have taken place in the Arab region since 2011,

---

1 Jamal Sanad Al-Suwaidi, *Events That Changed History* [in Arabic] (Abu Dhabi, 2018), pp. 215-224.

2 George Soros, *The Age of Fallibility: Consequences of the War on Terror*, (Public Affairs, 2006), pp. 137-138.

3 Jamal Sanad Al-Suwaidi, *Events That Changed History* [in Arabic] (Abu Dhabi, 2018), pp. 215-224.

4 For more details, see: Hasan Salem bin Salem, "Daesh and Transborder Terrorism," [in Arabic], *Derasat Series*, no. 11 (Riyadh: King Faisal Center for Islamic Research and Studies, 2016).

which have been labeled the Arab Spring.[1] Subsequently, the region entered a phase of "excessive terrorism,"[2] with the advent of political Islamic groups that used to conduct their activities secretly, mainly the Muslim Brotherhood. These groups, armed with religion,[3] took the center stage in the Arab world, and introduced a new dynamic to the people of the region, in order to hold the reins of power or spread chaos. Meanwhile, jihadi groups gained momentum with the emergence of ISIS, which declared the establishment of the Caliphate (Islamic State) in 2014 over huge areas of land in Syria and Iraq.[4] These developments opened the door for destruction, violence, and terrorism in Arab countries, extending to Egypt and Libya, among others. The core of the Western world was not spared, as it endured numerous terrorist attacks that

---

1 The term "Arab Spring" refers to the events witnessed in the Arab region from the end of 2010. They resulted in the toppling of some ruling regimes in Tunisia, Egypt, Libya, and Yemen as well as igniting civil conflicts as in the cases of Syria, Yemen, and Libya. The Western media dubbed it the "Arab Spring" in reference to the "Prague Spring," which describes the uprising by the people of Czechoslovakia, at the time, against the former Soviet Union in 1968. See: Musleh Khader Al-Juboori, *The Roots of Arab Oppression and the Arab Spring* [in Arabic] (Amman: Academics for Publishing and Distribution, 2013), p. 185.

2 Michael Rubin, "The age of hyper-terrorism and 'low cost' terrorism," The American Enterprise Institute, February 10, 2017, https://bit.ly/2wBwLd8

3 Jehad Odeh, *The Fall of the Brotherhood State* [in Arabic] (Cairo: Konooz Publishing and Distribution, 2013), p. 185.

4 Jamal Sanad Al-Suwaidi, *The Mirage*, (Abu Dhabi, 2015), pp. 265-269.

caused fear and destruction.[1] Arab societies promptly rejected political Islamic groups, mainly the Muslim Brotherhood, after unveiling their extremist truth; and Arab and international powers successfully terminated the Caliphate[2] of ISIS, and ended its "state"[3]; however, the threat posed by terrorism is not over yet, and may last for many more years, triggering further danger and destruction.[4]

The UAE was not spared from the changes that transformed the terror phenomenon, as the country was subject to its dangers and threats, yet it was vigilant against the plots of these archaic terrorist organizations, as was the case when a terrorist plot was foiled in 2012.[5] The UAE countered the Muslim Brotherhood's ideas, and unveiled the real motives behind the elements of the group inside

---

1 Jamal Sanad Al-Suwaidi, *Events That Changed History* [in Arabic] (Abu Dhabi, 2018), pp. 215-224.

2 Margaret Coker, Eric Schmitt, and Rukmini Callimachi, "With Loss of Its Caliphate, ISIS May Return to Guerrilla Roots," *New York Times*, October 18, 2017.

3 For more details on ISIS see: Jassem Mohammad, *Daesh, the Declaration of the Islamic State, and the Conflict over 'Al Bay'a'* [in Arabic] (Cairo: Al Maktab Al Arabi Lil Maaref, 2015).

4 Shamlan bin Abdullah Al-Mannaa'i, "The End of ISIS Does Not Mean the End of Terrorism" [in Arabic], *Asharq Al Awsat* (London), November 16, 2016.

5 Ahmad Qandeel, "Secret organization in the UAE: From the roots of conspiracy against the system until the verdict" [in Arabic], *Elaph*, July 19, 2013, http://elaph.com/Web/news/2013/7/821378.html. See also: Mohammad Basyuoni, "Withdrawal from Society: Will Isolationist Takfiri Groups Spread after ISIS Retreat?" *Future Center for Advanced Research and Studies*, December 1, 2016, https://bit.ly/2geo1V3

the country. These elements were closely linked to the international organization of the Muslim Brotherhood, which disregards the principles of patriotism and entitlements of citizenship.[1] The UAE has also been effectively engaged in all regional and international efforts aimed at fighting terrorism and extremist thought in the region and worldwide. It launched numerous significant initiatives nationally, in order to promote values of tolerance, shun extremist thought, and spread awareness about the serious dangers of these terrorist organizations and their backward ideology.[2]

The Middle East has also faced an equally hazardous challenge of civil wars and conflicts that have become one of the more risky characteristics of the region.[3] This danger is expected to intensify in the upcoming period, in light of some sects and ethnic groups' aspirations for independence,[4] the growth in strength of some armed organizations that have hijacked the decision-making process in their nation

---

1 Jamal Sanad Al-Suwaidi, *The Mirage*, (Abu Dhabi, 2015), p. 195.

2 For more on the UAE's efforts in combating terrorism and extremism, see the speech [in Arabic] by H.E. Ambassador Obaid Salem Al Zaabi, UAE Permanent Representative to the UN in Geneva, at the Geneva Conference on Preventing Violent Extremism, April 9, 2016, https://bit.ly/2qoJAnX

3 Ali Al-Deen Hilal, "The State of the Arab Nation (2014-2015): The Hurricane ...From Changing Regimes to Dissolving States" [in Arabic], *Arab Future Magazine*, no. 435 (Beirut, May 2015), p. 18.

4 Ahmad Sayyed Ahmad, "The Plight of the Arab National State" [in Arabic], *Al Ahram* (Cairo, September 20, 2017).

states[1] (such as Hezbollah in Lebanon, the Houthi rebels in Yemen, the Popular Mobilization militias in Iraq, and the many armed groups that have proliferated in Syria and Libya), and the increase in scale of religious, doctrinal, and sectarian tensions[2] that are taking on unprecedented dimensions.

There is no doubt these regional challenges require acute awareness at the UAE level, in order to face them within a comprehensive approach, taking into consideration numerous facts, of which I name three. First, the UAE's social stability is directly targeted by certain regional forces and terrorist organizations.[3] Second, the UAE society is a model of stability, unity, and cohesion in the region; thus, it is highly important to preserve and consolidate these characteristics. Third, the UAE is strongly and effectively engaged in the region's issues and developments.[4]

In this context, there are social dimensions that need to be fully grasped and addressed, most remarkably in

---

1 "The threat of sectarian militias and their role in Iran's expansion strategy" [in Arabic], *Nation Shield*, December 12, 2017, https://goo.gl/u9m7YJ

2 Mohammad Al-Shyookh, "Reflections of Sectarian Violence on National Unity" [in Arabic], *Middle East Online*, March 1, 2016, http://middle-east-online.com/?id=219222

3 Ahmad Ghallab, "The UAE: Rapid Steps toward War on Terror" [in Arabic], *Al Hayat* (London) November 28, 2014.

4 Ali Abu-Alreesh, "The UAE: A Regional and International Power" [in Arabic], *Al-Ittihad* (Abu Dhabi) March 2, 2017.

terms of the UAE's foreign military engagements,[1] which involve human sacrifices that leave a social impact. This is the case when members of the UAE Armed Forces fell as martyrs in the operation to restore legitimacy in Yemen, which demonstrated the strength of UAE society and its readiness to make such sacrifices. His Highness Sheikh Mohamed bin Zayed Al Nahyan, Crown Prince of Abu Dhabi and Deputy Supreme Commander of the UAE Armed Forces (may God protect him), expressed this notion in his statement on the 40th anniversary of the unification of the UAE Armed Forces, saying that, "Societies that lack the ability to defend themselves and the will to make sacrifices for their interests and sovereignty are fragile societies that cannot live with dignity in an age fraught with dangers, threats, and aggression. Over the past years, UAE society has proven itself to be solid, coherent, prepared to make sacrifices, and capable of understanding what it takes to prevent threats to the nation. All of this has been manifested in the support it has shown to its Armed Forces in the tasks they have undertaken in recent years, from assisting in foiling the conspiracy against the brotherly Kingdom of Bahrain in 2011, to taking part in the international coalition against

---

1 On the UAE military role abroad, see: Hussein Ibish, *The UAE's Evolving National Security Strategy* (Washington: Arab Gulf States Institute in Washington, 2017), pp. 28-34.

terrorism, to participating in the Arab Coalition to restore legitimacy in brotherly Yemen. The UAE people have also expressed their public pride in our nation's martyrs and solidarity with their families."[1]

Finally, the risks and challenges in the regional environment are in constant interaction, and all signs indicate that they will remain a source of threat to regional societies, including UAE society, over the coming years, and possibly decades.[2]

---

1 See: Statement by H.H. Sheikh Mohamed bin Zayed Al Nahyan, Crown Prince of Abu Dhabi and Deputy Supreme Commander of the UAE Armed Forces (may God protect him), on the 40th Anniversary of the Unification of the UAE Armed Forces, May 5, 2016, https://bit.ly/2MHRcQz

2 Sara Khalil, "Mathew Burrows' *Middle East 2020*: A forward-looking view of the region's pathways" [in Arabic], *International Politics* (Cairo, October 15, 2014), http://www.siyassa.org.eg/News/4923.aspx

3

Knowledge-based Economy: The Path toward the Post-Oil Era

"If this revenue (oil), which we talk about now, runs out, there are alternatives that can replace it. The first of these are the culture and knowledge that my country and people are enjoying now, the factories, and the industrial and agricultural projects."

Zayed bin Sultan Al Nahyan

W hen I first published the study *United Arab Emirates Society: A Future Perspective*[1] in 2003, the debate about the need for economic diversification and building a knowledge-based economy decoupled from crude oil, the price fluctuation was not as intense as it is now, especially in light of the decline in oil prices that began in 2014 and which recently rose to US$80 in May 2018.[2] These factors all indicate the beginning of the end of the oil era.[3] Nevertheless, it was a pioneering study in its call for a knowledge-based economy.[4] The ideas it offered in this regard, although they were presented more than a decade ago, seem acutely relevant to the nation's current economic orientations, which provide the recent framework for the preparations of the post-oil era.

---

1 Jamal Sanad Al-Suwaidi, *United Arab Emirates Society: A Future Perspective* [in Arabic], Emirates Lectures Series, no. 71 (Abu Dhabi: Emirates Center for Strategic Studies and Research, 2003).

2 Reuters, "Oil prices reach US$80 per barrel amid fears about Iranian supply" [in Arabic], May 17, 2018.

3 Sukina Meshekhis, "The End of the Oil Age" [in Arabic], *Al Arab* (London), January 4, 2016. See also: David Goodstein, *Out of Gas: The End of the Age of Oil* (New York: W.W. Norton & Company, 2005), pp. 117-120. For more details on the issue of the end of the oil age see: Colin Campbell et al., *The End of the Age of Oil: Necessary Measures for the Future* [in Arabic] (Kuwait: National Council for Culture, Arts, and Letters, September 2004).

4 Jamal Sanad Al-Suwaidi, *United Arab Emirates Society: A Future Perspective* [in Arabic], Emirates Lectures Series, no. 71 (Abu Dhabi: Emirates Center for Strategic Studies and Research, 2003), p. 23.

The study drew attention to the fact that the UAE Government depends on crude oil as a source of revenue, which exposes the state budget to risks from the instability and volatility of the global oil markets.[1] Additionally, the rapid advancements in information and communications technology changed the rules of international trade and economic activity in many countries of the world.[2] The wealth of a nation no longer depends on its industrial and commodity production capacity, but rather on its capability to produce knowledge.[3] This necessitates preparing human resources equipped with the relevant skills and expertise so that they may depend more on knowledge than on physical effort.[4]

The study predicted that the transition to a knowledge-based economy would lead to a transformation in the nature of economic power[5] and the traditional elements of production (labor force, production tools, and

---

1 Jamal Sanad Al-Suwaidi, *United Arab Emirates Society: A Future Perspective* [in Arabic], Emirates Lectures Series, no. 71 (Abu Dhabi: Emirates Center for Strategic Studies and Research, 2003), p. 28.

2 Angela Abell and Nigel Oxbrow, *Competing with Knowledge* (London: Library Association Publishing, 2001), p. 4.

3 Alan Burton-Jones, *Knowledge Capitalism: Business, Work and Learning in the New Economy* (Oxford: Oxford University Press, 1999), p. 12. See also: Mustafa Yousef Kafi, *E-Learning and Knowledge Economy* [in Arabic] (Damascus: Raslan Publishing House, 2009), p. 178.

4 "Toward the Knowledge Society," Council for Scientific Research, Issue 1: The Arab Knowledge Society and Its Role in Development" [in Arabic] (Riyadh: Scientific Research Council, King Abdulaziz University), p. 7.

5 Alan Burton-Jones, *Knowledge Capitalism: Business, Work and Learning in the New Economy* (Oxford: Oxford University Press, 1999), p. 3.

capital), while knowledge capital would start to challenge
all other forms of capital.[1] It is a reality we are experiencing
today. States that possess knowledge and which have
heavily invested in the knowledge-based economy have
succeeded in reinforcing their economic capabilities in an
unprecedented manner. Knowledge capital has become the
dominant factor, as global e-commerce between companies,
on the one hand, and companies and consumers, on the
other, exceeded US$27 trillion in 2016.[2] Information
technology companies now top the list of the most valuable
businesses in the world;[3] Apple's market value in 2018
reached one trillion dollars.[4]

According to the *United Arab Emirates Society: A
Future Perspective* study,[5] the changes in the nature of the
world economy pose many challenges to the UAE.
Therefore, we should elaborate on three of these challenges.
The **first** is the creation of human capital that is capable of

---

1 Alan Burton-Jones, *Knowledge Capitalism: Business, Work and Learning in the New Economy* (Oxford: Oxford University Press, 1999), p. 22.

2 United States International Trade Commission, "Global Digital Trade 1: Market Opportunities and Key Foreign Trade Restrictions," USITC Publication 4716, August 2017, p. 147.

3 Kristin Stoller, "The World's Largest Tech Companies 2017: Apple and Samsung Lead, Facebook Rises," *Forbes*, May 24, 2017, https://bit.ly/2GRs5UB

4 Ian Bogost, "Apple Is Worth One Trillion Dollars," The Atlantic, August 2, 2018, https://bit.ly/2OEENKo

5 Jamal Sanad Al-Suwaidi, *United Arab Emirates Society: A Future Perspective* [in Arabic], Emirates Lectures Series, no. 71 (Abu Dhabi: Emirates Center for Strategic Studies and Research, 2003), p. 29.

dealing with knowledge-based work systems and under-standing the aspects of the global information revolution. The **second** is the enactment of necessary legislation to regulate the labor market, which is based on pro-fessionalism and knowledge management, and the **third** is the restructuring of the national economy in terms of the diversification of the economic base to fit the output of the knowledge-based economy.

Building an Emirati strategy of economic diversifi-cation and a knowledge-based economy firstly requires identifying and addressing the weaknesses of the economy as well as exploiting and utilizing its strengths.[1] In this context, the study defines the strengths[2] in terms of: the existence of vast oil and gas reserves (estimated at about 5.7 percent of global oil reserves[3] and 3.3 percent of the world's natural gas reserves);[4] the presence of solid and modern infrastructure; continued growth in the non-oil commodities export sector; the existence of private sector investments in

---

1 Emirates Center for Strategic Studies and Research, Project on Economic Diversification in the United Arab Emirates [in Arabic], Part 1, Executive Summary, unpublished study, (Abu Dhabi, 2001), p. 10.

2 Jamal Sanad Al-Suwaidi, *United Arab Emirates Society: A Future Perspective* [in Arabic], Emirates Lectures Series, no. 71 (Abu Dhabi: Emirates Center for Strategic Studies and Research, 2003), p. 30.

3 "BP Statistical Review of World Energy," BP, June 2017, https://on.bp.com/2IIOAeS

4 "BP Statistical Review of World Energy," BP, June 2016, p. 20, https://on.bp.com/2bSW4Mf

significant economic activities; the labor force shift toward service sectors; the favorable strategic location of the country; the modern financial and banking services available, and other factors that enhance the nation's economic competitiveness.

The study identified the following weaknesses:[1] The demand for manufactured imports was growing at a rate higher than the expansion of non-oil exports, causing pressure on the trade balance and stagnation of government revenues. This trade imbalance may grow even more in the future (because of the drop in oil prices); the increase in consumption and decrease in production in some sectors impact the reserve capacity of the economy; and the presence of unskilled laborers reinforces the continued low production level of the labor force in general.

The study did not just call for economic diversification, nor did it just focus on the aspects of strength and weakness in the UAE economy. It also offers a specific vision of the strategy of economic diversification that was based on six industrial clusters that are of critical importance to the UAE economy, and which represent opportunities to diversify the UAE economy.

---

1 Jamal Sanad Al-Suwaidi, *United Arab Emirates Society: A Future Perspective* [in Arabic], Emirates Lectures Series, no. 71 (Abu Dhabi: Emirates Center for Strategic Studies and Research, 2003), pp. 30-31.

Namely, these are: oil and gas, financial services, information technology, the pharmaceutical industry, installation and maintenance services, and the fishing and marine industry.[1] Moreover, the study underscored the importance of focusing on export industries, especially in the sectors of high-tech manufacturing, value-added services, transportation services, and natural resource-based industries, among others.[2]

Much has happened to the UAE economy since the first edition of the study, which was published in 2003, especially in relation to economic diversification and the knowledge-based economy. What is important from my point of view, however, is that the UAE leadership was proactive in realizing that the beginning of the end of the oil era had already begun,[3] and accordingly, it was important to admit this and work on a plan for the future. His Highness Sheikh Mohamed bin Zayed Al Nahyan, Crown Prince of Abu Dhabi and Deputy Supreme Commander of the UAE Armed Forces (may God protect him), has actually led the way in elaborating on the post-oil era and

---

1 Emirates Center for Strategic Studies and Research, Project on Economic Diversification in the United Arab Emirates [in Arabic], Part 1, Executive Summary, unpublished study, (Abu Dhabi, 2001), p. 6.

2 Ibid., p. 7.

3 Mohammed Al-Hammadi, "The UAE is ready for the post-oil era" [in Arabic], *Al-Ittihad* (Abu Dhabi), January 31, 2016.

the need to be prepared through investing in the education sector.[1]

The economies of the oil-producing countries depend on oil revenues. Unfortunately, for many years some of these countries ignored the possibility that the oil era would end,[2] whether in terms of a huge decline in oil prices or the depletion of oil reserves over time. It is high time that the oil-producing countries, especially those in the GCC, acknowledge that the countdown to the post-oil era has already started.[3] This is not only because the resource of oil will be depleted by virtue of the passage of time, but also because we are witnessing the era of inexpensive oil.[4] Furthermore, the underlying reasons for declining oil prices since 2014 are neither exceptional nor temporary, as was the case in the past; instead, there are structural causes[5] relating to a number of factors:

---

1 Mohamed bin Zayed, "Today, we think and plan for the next 50 years and for the good of the generations" [in Arabic], *Al Bayan* (Dubai), February 10, 2015.

2 Salam Al-Shamma, "The technological progress refutes the argument of the end of the Oil Age," [in Arabic], *Al Arab* (London), June 19, 2017.

3 A. C. Grayling, "Prepare for the post-oil era," *The Guardian*, March 14, 2007. https://www.theguardian.com/commentisfree/2007/mar/14/bythistimenextyear

4 Mohamed A. El-Erian, "This era of low-cost oil is different," *Bloomberg*, December 29, 2014, https://www.bloomberg.com/view/articles/2014-12-29/this-era-of-lowcost-oil-is-different.

5 Rania Marzouq, "The Geopolitical Implications of Low Oil Prices" [in Arabic], *International Politics* (Cairo), November 18, 2014, http:// www. siyassa.org.eg/News/4995.aspx.

First is an increase in oil discoveries worldwide,[1] with the emergence of several new exporters in the global oil market, intensified competition for market share, and the resulting price-dumping policy. At the same time, the US has disregarded environmental considerations (such as its withdrawal from the Paris Climate Agreement)[2] and has moved toward more investments in oil exploration.[3]

Second, shale oil, particularly in the US, has begun to compete with traditional oil production,[4] which cannot be underestimated, as was the case in the past. Despite falling oil prices, shale oil has shown resilience in the market because of the modern technologies that helped producers lower drilling and production costs.[5] If the US

---

1 "New Oil Finds around the Globe: Will the U.S. Capitalize on Its Oil Resources?" The Institute for Energy Research (IER), https://bit.ly/2MKZOpJ

2 "Trump announces withdrawal from Paris Climate Agreement to protect USA and its people" [in Arabic], *CNN*, June 1, 2017, https://arabic.cnn.com/world/2017/06/01/trump-paris-climate-decision

3 Hadi Fathallah, "Trump's impact on the global financial markets: increased fragility"[in Arabic], Carnegie Endowment for International Peace, November 10, 2016, http://carnegieendowment.org/sada/65105

4 Mohammed El-Erian, *The Available Game...Disorder of Central Banks and Averting the next Collapse* [translated into Arabic by Mustafa Mahmoud] (Cairo: Dar Al Kotob Khan, 2018), p. 268.

5 Mohamed Ibrahim El Sakka, "Shale oil revolution ... once again" [in Arabic], *Al Eqtisadya* (Riyadh), May 23, 2014. See also: International Monetary Fund, "World Economic Outlook, Seeking Sustainable Growth: Short-Term Recovery, Long-Term Challenges" [in Arabic] (Washington, 2017), pp. 54-61, https://bit.ly/2GPtpLD

becomes a major oil producer and exporter, it is predicted that the Gulf region, which includes the UAE, would lose its significance to the US, which could also emerge as a competitor in the Asian markets.

Third, the substantial technological advancements in the search for alternatives to oil, especially in the areas of electricity, nuclear energy, renewable energy, and so on.[1]

Fourth, the remarkable technological progress in the field of rationalizing and reducing energy consumption in general.[2]

In light of the aforementioned factors, economic diversification is no longer one of the options on the table; rather, it has become both an imperative and an existential question. One of the positive indicators in this regard is that the GCC countries have become aware of this reality and are acting accordingly, albeit to varying degrees. The UAE remains a pioneer in this field because it started

---

1   Hani Abdel Kader Amara, *Energy and the Age of Power* [in Arabic] (Amman: Dar Ghaida' Publishing and Distribution, 2011) p. 18. See also: "Oil and the Alternative Energy Resources" [in Arabic], *Akhbar Al Saah* (Abu Dhabi: Emirates Center for Strategic Studies and Research, January 23, 2002).

2   Economic and Social Commission for Western Asia (ESCWA), "Rationalizing and Improving Energy and Efficiency in the Higher Sectors of Energy Generation in Selected ESCWA Member States" [in Arabic], 2007, pp. 14-33, https://www.uncclearn.org/sites/default/files/inventory/unescwa07. pdf

earlier and possessed the courage and self-confidence to plan for an economic future that is independent of oil.

A brief examination of the UAE's development over the past decade confirms the farsighted development visions adopted by the country's leadership. The leaders have placed great importance on providing the foundations and requirements for the transition to a knowledge-based economy and achieving sustainable economic development, whether through strategic visions or executive plans and policies.[1]

The goal of building a "diversified and flexible knowledge-based economy powered by skilled Emiratis and strengthened by world-class talents to ensure long-term prosperity for the UAE"[2] was one of the six main pillars of UAE Vision 2021.[3] This vision stresses the

---

1   Nowzad A. Alhiti, "Knowledge-based Economy in the United Arab Emirates: An Analytical Study" [in Arabic], *Almanhal*, https://platform.almanhal.com/Reader/2/105209.

2   "United in Knowledge," UAE Vision 2021 [in Arabic], https://bit.ly/ 2yIzV31.

3   UAE Vision 2021 was launched by H.H. Sheikh Mohammed bin Rashid Al Maktoum, Vice President and Prime Minister of the UAE and Ruler of Dubai (may God protect him), at the closing of a Cabinet meeting in 2010. The Vision aims to make the UAE among the best countries in the world by the Golden Jubilee of the Union. In order to translate the Vision into reality, its pillars have been mapped into six national priorities, which represent the key focus sectors of government action in the coming years. It has been divided into four main themes: united in responsibility, united in destiny, united in knowledge, and united in prosperity. See: "UAE Vision 2021," https://bit. ly/2PtvtJa

importance of realizing this goal through encouraging innovation, research, science, and technology, and creating an entrepreneurial environment conducive to the growth of a knowledge-based economy, while nurturing the full potential of Emirati human capital to deal with this knowledge-based economic transition.

Abu Dhabi Economic Vision 2030, issued in November 2008, defined the priorities of the emirate's economic policy in building "Abu Dhabi as a sustainable, diversified, high-value-added economy that encourages enterprises and entrepreneurship and is well integrated in the global economy, leading to better opportunities for all."[1] The UAE leadership has approved several initiatives, policies, and national projects to realize this ambitious economic vision.

The most prominent of these initiatives, for example, was the declaration of the UAE National Agenda[2] in January 2014 to translate the UAE Vision 2021 into a practical reality over the seven-year period. The National Agenda includes a set of national indicators in the sectors of education, healthcare, economy, policies, security, housing, infrastructure, and government services. These

---

1   "Abu Dhabi Economic Vision 2030" [in Arabic], November 2008, p. 17, https://www.ecouncil.ae/Publications/economic-vision-2030-full-version.pdf.

2   "Mohammed bin Rashid launches the National Agenda for the coming years" [in Arabic], *Al-Ittihad* (Abu Dhabi), January 14, 2014.

indicators aim at continuing efforts to achieve this target and build the knowledge-based economy.[1] In October 2014, the National Innovation Strategy[2] was launched with the aim of making the UAE one of the most innovative nations in the world within seven years. This strategy aims to stimulate innovation in the main sectors of importance to the state's planning for the future: renewable energy, transport, education, health, technology, water, and space.

Another initiative is the approval of the Science, Technology, and Innovation Policy in the UAE[3] in 2015. It includes 100 initiatives, with a total investment volume of AED 300 billion,[4] which aim to prepare UAE society for the post-oil era. In September 2017, the UAE government launched the UAE Strategy for the Fourth Industrial Revolution (4IR),[5] and the 4IR Council was established. This strategy aims to strengthen the UAE's position as a global hub for the 4IR and to increase its

---

1 Ahmed Majid, *Innovation Enhancement Mechanisms in the UAE* [in Arabic], UAE Ministry of Economy, 2017, p. 5, https://goo.gl/4b1DzX

2 "National Innovation Strategy" [in Arabic], UAE Ministry of Cabinet Affairs and the Future website, 2015, https://bit.ly/2t762nM.

3 "Science, Technology & Innovation Policy in the UAE" [in Arabic], UAE Ministry of Cabinet Affairs and the Future, November 2015, https://bit.ly/2v40xK5.

4 Ahmed Majid, *Innovation Enhancement Mechanisms in the UAE* [in Arabic], UAE Ministry of Economy, 2017, p. 6, https://goo.gl/4b1DzX

5 "The UAE Strategy for the Fourth Industrial Revolution," Official Portal of the UAE Government, https://bit.ly/2MwhTYp

contribution to the creation of a competitive national economy based on knowledge, innovation, and future technologies, as well as applications that merge physical, digital, and biological technologies.

The UAE transitioned from the e-government[1] phase, which was declared in 2000, to the Smart Government[2] phase, which was initiated by His Highness Sheikh Mohammed bin Rashid Al Maktoum, Vice President and Prime Minister of the UAE and Ruler of Dubai (may God protect him), in May 2013. It will enable society's members to access government services through their smartphones around the clock.

The UAE has entered the global space exploration race by sending the Hope Probe[3] to explore Mars. In June 2018, His Highness Sheikh Mohammed bin Rashid Al Maktoum, Vice President and Prime Minister of the UAE and Ruler of Dubai (may God protect him), announced that the UAE had signed a historical agreement to send the first Emirati astronaut to the International Space Station in April 2019.[4] On September 3, 2018, the names of Hazza

---

1   Abdullah Al-Awadhi, "The UAE's Smart Government Initiative" [in Arabic], Emirates Center for Strategic Studies and Research, June 18, 2013, http://www.ecssr.ac.ae/ECSSR/print/ft.jsp?lang=ar&ftId=/FeatureTopic/Abdullah_AlAwadhi/FeatureTopic_1695.xml

2   Amna Al-Kutubi, "Smart government...The UAE's path toward the future" [in Arabic], *Al-Ittihad* (Abu Dhabi), April 27, 2017.

3   "Hope Probe," UAE Space Agency, https://bit.ly/2LND7Mb.

4   "UAE, Russia sign deal to send first Emirati into space" [in Arabic], *Emarat Alyoum* (Dubai), June 20, 2018.

Ali Al-Mansouri and Sultan Saif Al-Neyadi were revealed as the first two Emirati astronauts. They were selected, in collaboration with the Russian Space Agency, Roscosmos, from over 4,000 candidates who applied for the UAE Astronaut Program, which aims to prepare and send Emirati astronauts to space to carry out scientific missions.[1]

In line with this farsighted vision, the UAE Government launched the UAE Centennial Plan 2071[2] in March 2017, which offers a clear map for long-term government work to fortify the country's reputation and its soft power.[3] The UAE Centennial Plan will focus on four main objectives:[4]

- **The first** is to develop a flexible government with farsighted leadership and a clear vision that prioritizes the people and spreads positive messages to the world.

- **The second** is to invest in education, focusing on advanced science and technology and establishing professionalism and ethics in educational institutions to produce open-minded graduates who are well-informed about the world's experiences.

---

1 "UAE announces names of its first astronauts," *Khaleej Times* (Sharjah), September 4, 2018.

2 "Mohammed bin Rashid launches 'UAE Centennial Plan 2071' to make UAE the best in the world" [in Arabic], *Al-Ittihad* (Abu Dhabi), March 23, 2017.

3 "Future," Official Portal of the UAE Government, https://bit.ly/2LNcNlr

4 "Mohammed bin Rashid launches 'UAE Centennial Plan 2071' to fortify the UAE's reputation and its soft power" [in Arabic], *Al Bayan* (Dubai), March 23, 2017.

- **The third** is to establish a diversified knowledge-based economy that competes with the best economies in the world.

- **The fourth** is to consolidate the values of tolerance, social cohesion, and respect in society within a comprehensive development plan to make the UAE the best country in the world by 2071.

In October 2017, the UAE Strategy for Artificial Intelligence (AI)[1] was launched as the first project in the UAE Centennial Plan 2071. The strategy aims to make the UAE the first in the field of AI investments in various sectors globally, while also creating a vital new market with high economic value in the region, supporting private sector initiatives, and increasing productivity. It also aims to build a solid research development base while fully utilizing artificial intelligence (AI) methods in services and data analysis by 2031.[2]

To realize its vision to transform the traditional oil-based economy to a diversified and knowledge-based one, the UAE has launched strategies and initiatives in recent years, which aim to move Emirati society toward a "knowledge society"[3] that can cope with the accelerated

---

1 "UAE Strategy for Artificial Intelligence (AI)," http://www.uaeai.ae/en/

2 "Mohammed bin Rashid launches the UAE Strategy for Artificial Intelligence (AI)" [in Arabic], *Emarat Alyoum* (Dubai), October 17, 2017.

3 Mohammed Ibrahim, "UAE heading toward a knowledge society" [in Arabic], *Al Khaleej* (Sharjah), September 10, 2016.

global advancement in knowledge, culture, and technology. They adhere to our leadership's farsighted vision about the rapidly accelerating changes, both regionally and internationally. In addition, they demonstrate the leadership's eagerness, not only to adapt to these changes, but also to place the UAE at the forefront in the global race toward the future and to consolidate the UAE's leading development model worldwide.

Furthermore, the strategies and initiatives adopted by the UAE reiterate the credibility and significance of the argument I presented 15 years ago in the study *United Arab Emirates Society: A Future Perspective*,[1] which stresses the importance of economic diversification and preparation for the post-oil era by focusing on fulfilling the requirements for shifting to the world of knowledge-based economies, especially in light of the indicators that emphasize the substantial increase of the knowledge component in the economy.[2]

---

1 Jamal Sanad Al-Suwaidi, *United Arab Emirates Society: A Future Perspective* [in Arabic], Emirates Lectures Series, no. 71 (Abu Dhabi: Emirates Center for Strategic Studies and Research, 2003).

2 Ali Al-Salmi, *Management in the Age of Knowledge and Globalization* [in Arabic] (Cairo: Sama Publishing Production, and Distribution, 2014), p. 80.

4

Education and the Building of National Capacities and Human Resources

"Thanks to excellent education, we can provide a generation of citizens capable of building factories and managing projects that have been launched all over the country."

Zayed bin Sultan Al Nahyan

C ertain studies that discuss education and academic research and their links to human development, and development in general, adopt a quantitative approach, by focusing on the number of schools and universities as well as the number of enrolled students and graduates of both sexes, etc. Yet, *United Arab Emirates Society: A Future Perspective*,[1] which explores the quantitative growth in UAE education by listing the accumulated number of schools, universities, institutes, and graduates[2] since the establishment of the country in 1971, focuses primarily on the qualitative aspects, concerning the quality of education in the country and examining its ability to meet the requirements of development in the age of knowledge, and to effectively respond to modern changes in the field of development, mainly regarding the concepts of human development,[3] intellectual development,[4] and the knowledge-based economy,[5] among others.

---

1 Jamal Sanad Al-Suwaidi, *United Arab Emirates Society: A Future Perspective* [in Arabic], Emirates Lectures Series, no. 71 (Abu Dhabi: Emirates Center for Strategic Studies and Research, 2003).

2 Ibid., pp. 34-36.

3 For a definition of human development, see: Abdulkareem Ahmad Jameel, *Modern Human Development* [in Arabic] (Amman: Dar Al Janadriyyah for Publishing and Distribution, 2017), pp. 7-11.

4 For a definition of intellectual development, see: Sa'doun Hmoud Al-Rbei'awi and Hussein Waleed Abbas, *Intellectual Capital* [in Arabic] (Amman: Dar Ghaida' Publishing and Distribution, 2015).

5 For a definition of the knowledge economy see: Jamal Dawood Salman, *Knowledge Economy* [in Arabic] (Amman: Dar Al-Yazouri for Publishing and Distribution, 2012).

In fact, the emphasis on this aspect deserves more attention, follow up, and discussion, since the decisive indicator of countries' competitive capabilities in the field of education is the quality, rather than the quantity, of education.

In this context, the study[1] sheds light on numerous aspects and facts, including:

1. The budget the UAE allocates for public education is low compared to that of the developed countries. The study refers in this regard to statistics included in the Human Development Report published by the United Nations Development Program in 2002,[2] (the study was first published in 2003). The statistics indicate that the UAE spent 1.7 percent of its gross domestic product (GDP) on education from 1995 to 1997,[3] while countries that have advanced in the field of human development like Sweden and Norway spent respectively 8.3 percent and 7.7 percent of their GDP on education.[4] The recent years that followed the

---

1   Jamal Sanad Al-Suwaidi, *United Arab Emirates Society: A Future Perspective* [in Arabic], Emirates Lectures Series, no. 71 (Abu Dhabi: Emirates Center for Strategic Studies and Research, 2003).

2   See: "Human Development Report 2002," United Nations Development Programme, United Nations, http://bit.ly/1vGMTQt

3   Jamal Sanad Al-Suwaidi, *United Arab Emirates Society: A Future Perspective* [in Arabic], Emirates Lectures Series, no. 71 (Abu Dhabi: Emirates Center for Strategic Studies and Research, 2003), p. 36.

4   Ibid. p. 36.

publication of this study have undoubtedly witnessed great strides regarding the UAE's expenditure on education; for instance, the budget allocated for the education sector in 2007 represented 20.5 percent of the overall budget.[1]

However, the central point made in this study, regarding the UAE's suboptimal expenditure on education, is still persistent; because the key standard remains the ratio to GDP, and not to the overall budget, of public expenditure on education.

Table 4-1

Ratio to GDP of Public Expenditure on Education in the UAE Compared to Other Countries

Country	Percentage
UAE	1.10
Malaysia	5.12
Korea	4.93
Australia	5.26
Japan	3.53

Source: World Talent Report 2016, Institute for Management Development, Switzerland, November 2016.

---

1 "UAE Cabinet approves AED 248 billion federal budget for 2017-2021," *Gulf News* (Dubai), October 30, 2016, https://bit.ly/2wptLRc

The World Talent Report 2016,[1] published by the Institute for Management Development in Switzerland, indicates that the Ratio to GDP of the UAE public expenditure on education is 1.10 percent, while this percentage reaches 5.12 percent, 4.93 percent, 5.26 percent, and 3.53 percent in Malaysia, Korea, Australia, and Japan[2] respectively, as shown in Table 4-1, above.

Table 4-2
Ratio to GDP of Public Expenditure

Rank	Country	Percentage
1	Iceland	7.6
2	Denmark	7.6
3	South Africa	7.3
4	Ukraine	7.2
5	Portugal	6.8
6	Sweden	6.6
7	Belgium	6.4
8	Finland	6.4
9	Brazil	6.4
10	Israel	6.3

Source: World Talent Report 2016, Institute for Management Development, Switzerland, November 2016.

---

1 See: Institute for Management Development, "IMD World Talent Report 2016," Switzerland, November 2016, https://bit.ly/2tG19BH

2 Ibid.

It is important to note that the ratio to GDP of the UAE public expenditure for the period 1995-1997 (1.7 percent) is almost the same for the period 2015-2016 (1.10 percent), even though the interval between the two periods is approximately 20 years long. This period witnessed massive changes in the education sector nationally, regionally, and internationally, which underlines the urgent need to adopt a new vision for education in the UAE, in order to address this sector in the appropriate way, through clear programs, policies, and strategies, because this sector is the engine of the nation's advancement, and the solid foundation on which to rely in preparation for the post-oil era, as was stressed in the vision of His Highness Sheikh Mohamed bin Zayed Al Nahyan, Crown Prince of Abu Dhabi and Deputy Supreme Commander of the UAE Armed Forces (may God protect him).[1]

In a presentation I made in 1998 on the sidelines of the Emirates Center for Strategic Studies and Research's Fourth Annual Conference, titled 'Challenges of the Next Millennium: Education and Development of Human Resources,' I said, "It is time we put our

---

1 "The vision of Mohamed bin Zayed sets the foundations for a modern education that meets the ambitions of the UAE," [in Arabic], *Emarat Al-Youm* (Dubai), January 12, 2017.

resources in the right place by investing in the educational process. Education is the basis through which we may gain a generation or lose it. Therefore, if we do not lay strong foundations to address the 21st century's challenges, by investing in education, we will certainly lose the future generation."[1] After almost 20 years, world developments have demonstrated that education has become the principal standard to achieve progress, distinguish between countries, create wealth, and build power in the international arena.

2. The growing number of high school graduates has led to the proliferation of private higher education institutions, granting further chances to children of UAE residents to stay in the country. Moreover, the residents that graduated from private universities are competing with Emirati graduates for the available job opportunities; something that has contributed to a deepening of the unbalanced demographic structure.[2] In fact, the increasing number of private higher education institutions in the UAE (65 private higher education institutions out of 76 higher education institutions,

---

1 You can listen to this dialogue on: https://www.facebook.com/jamalsanad alsuwaidi/videos/1472598089495311.

2 Jamal Sanad Al-Suwaidi, *United Arab Emirates Society: A Future Perspective* [in Arabic], Emirates Lectures Series, no. 71 (Abu Dhabi: Emirates Center for Strategic Studies and Research, 2003), p. 37.

according to statistics issued by the Ministry of Education)[1] has both positive and negative implications. On the one hand, this has a positive impact on the overall educational process, mainly in terms of expanding education options for students, and injecting new blood into the UAE educational process, most evidently as branches of foreign universities and institutes have increased in recent years.[2] On the other hand, the adverse aspects are manifested, for example, in the case of an American university that grants a master's degree in physical education in Arabic. Moreover, the low level of competence of the outputs of some private higher education institutions, as well as the adopted curricula and the granted certificates, are among the existing problems that need to be addressed, not by rejecting these institutions, rather by making

---

1 For more details, see the UAE Ministry of Education website, https://www. moe.gov.ae/en/OpenData/Pages/ReportsAndStatistics.aspx

2 Statistics for 2016 indicate that the United Arab Emirates hosts 31 branches of foreign higher education institutions, see: The Observatory on Borderless Higher Education, "International Branch Campuses Trends and Developments, 2016," http://www.obhe.ac.uk/documents/download?id=1049. The statistics for 2013 indicated that the UAE ranked first in the world in terms of the number of branches of foreign universities with a total of up to 35 branches, followed by China and Singapore. See also: Jason E. Lane, "The Impact of Branches of Foreign Universities in the UAE," in *The Future of Education in the UAE: Innovation and Knowledge Production* (Abu Dhabi: Emirates Center for Strategic Studies and Research, 2014), p. 129.

private higher education a real contribution to the education sector in the UAE.

There are some authorities that control quality in the private higher education institutions in the UAE, including the Commission for Academic Accreditation, established in 1999 to assure that these institutions and their academic programs are in line with international standards, and to prepare and implement quality standards according to which the private higher education institutions and scientific programs are authorized and accredited.[1] There is also the National Qualifications Authority, established in 2010 to set up regulations and standards for the qualifications of higher, public, technical, and vocational education and to provide the equivalence for those qualifications.[2]

However, specialized studies refer to problems and quality gaps regarding private higher education in the UAE, especially in light of the limited supervision over, and assessment of, private educational institutions in the free zones, the reliance on part-time employees in some institutions, and problems ensuing from the

---

1 See: Commission for Academic Accreditation (CAA), https://bit.ly/ 2BNOTGz

2 For more details, see: The National Qualifications Authority website, https:// www.nqa.gov.ae/en/pages/home.aspx

accreditation process of the certificate issued by these institutions and the like.[1]

3. The educational outputs do not match the requirements of the UAE labor market,[2] which constitutes a real problem that persists despite the efforts the government has exerted to address it. In fact, addressing this problem is not the responsibility of the Ministry of Education or the government alone; rather, it is a shared responsibility that involves society, family, media outlets, education institutions, and the private sector. This would motivate students to opt for the academic branches required for the advancement of the development process, mainly in the fields of applied sciences and technology. It would also help change students' traditional perception of education as a means to join the public sector upon graduation.[3]

The role of the private sector in this regard is highly important, in terms of the support provided by private

---

1   Robin Dada, "The UAE: A Regional Center for Education" [in Arabic], in *Education and Development: Investing in the Future* (Abu Dhabi: Emirates Center for Strategic Studies and Research, 2017) p. 110.

2   Abdullah Al-Raisi, "The Development Dimension of Education in the UAE" [in Arabic], in *Education and Development: Investing in the Future* (Abu Dhabi: Emirates Center for Strategic Studies and Research, 2017) p. 40.

3   In an unpublished poll by the Emirates Center for Strategic Studies and Research in 2018, on "Position of the UAE citizens on the education system and the job market," 72.9 percent of respondents said that they prefer to join government jobs or jobs in the military sector.

companies and institutions to educational and research university programs that meet labor market needs.[1] Higher institutions in the UAE are also required to keep abreast of new developments in the labor market and future jobs, so that they can develop their educational programs accordingly.[2]

Moreover, the study[3] highlights certain steps that the UAE has actually started to implement to keep pace with global developments in the fields of technology, information, and communication. The UAE is learning from new concepts and characteristics of education systems adopted in the developed world, mainly in terms of curricula, teaching methods, and school buildings, among others; and it is spreading the characteristics of modern education such as the promotion of innovation, creativity,

---

1 For more details on the role of the private sector in this regard, see: Barbara Harold, "The Role of the Private Sector in Supporting Research," in *Education and Development: Toward a Modern Education System in the UAE*, (Abu Dhabi: Emirates Center for Strategic Studies and Research, 2018), pp. 51-74.

2 The trends revealed by the participants in the Abu Dhabi Job Fair 2016 show the future aspects of the job market that require attention by the higher education institutions in the country, namely: all branches of engineering, health sciences, renewable energy, earth sciences, environmental and water majors, teaching, banking majors, and marketing. See: "8 specializations for the job market in the next 10 years" [in Arabic], *Emarat Al-Youm* (Dubai), February 3, 2016.

3 Jamal Sanad Al-Suwaidi, *United Arab Emirates Society: A Future Perspective* [in Arabic], Emirates Lectures Series, no. 71 (Abu Dhabi: Emirates Center for Strategic Studies and Research, 2003), pp. 37-39.

and continuous education; and meeting the needs of the technological revolution.

The study matches education with academic research, thus the better education (mainly higher education) is developed, the more competent scientific researchers become. In this context, the study touches on a highly significant issue, not only in the UAE, but also in the Arab region as a whole, which is the inadequate funding allocated for academic research compared to developed countries or those that have made major strides toward development.

In this context, statistics indicate that the ratio to GDP of academic research in the UAE public expenditure is still below 1 percent (0.87 percent), while this ratio reaches 4.27 percent, 2.88 percent, and 1.70 percent in Israel, Germany, and Britain respectively, according to 2015 World Bank statistics.[1] Therefore, the first step toward successful UAE plans in the fields of innovation, space, technology production, and Emiratization, is to increase financial allocations for academic research, as is the case in developed countries and those that have successfully caught up with them, including South Korea, Malaysia, Singapore, and the like.

---

1 See: "Research and development expenditure," World Bank website, https://bit.ly/2HqM9OL

The source of hope in this regard is that the UAE leadership is profoundly aware of this issue, as clearly manifested in the constant emphasis of His Highness Sheikh Mohamed bin Zayed Al Nahyan, Crown Prince of Abu Dhabi and Deputy Supreme Commander of the UAE Armed Forces (may God protect him), on the importance and priority of scientific research in the national development strategy.[1]

Within this context, the UAE launched the National Innovation Strategy in 2014,[2] and the Science, Technology, and Innovation Policy in the UAE in 2015,[3] which aim to increase three fold the ratio to GDP of academic research through public expenditure. *United Arab Emirates Society: A Future Perspective*[4] provides a framework for academic research in the UAE, based on four points. First, defining priorities for academic research in light of the local, regional, and global needs; in other words, the trends for academic research have to correspond to domestic development needs as well as the issues and contents of the

---

1 "Mohammad bin Zayed encourages scientific research," *Gulf News* (Dubai), May 9, 2017. https://bit.ly/2PE4QC9

2 See: "The National Innovation Strategy," Official Portal of the UAE Government, 2015, https://bit.ly/2Nj0j6t

3 See: "Science, Technology & Innovation Policy," Ministry of Cabinet Affairs and the Future, November 6, 2015, https://bit.ly/2MwEnsr

4 Jamal Sanad Al-Suwaidi, *United Arab Emirates Society: A Future Perspective* [in Arabic], Emirates Lectures Series, no. 71 (Abu Dhabi: Emirates Center for Strategic Studies and Research, 2003)

development process, regionally and globally. Second, the accumulation, spread, and Emiratization of knowledge. Third, the mobilization of public and private resources to finance academic research. This step is highly important, because the promotion of the academic research system is not the responsibility of the government alone, but is rather shared with the private sector as well, as is the case in the developed world. Fourth, the development of human resources in the field of academic research, which does not solely rely on financial support, modern equipment and institutions, but also requires qualified human resources.[1]

In this context, the role of education in building local human capabilities is primarily related to the role of education in human development. As such, it is not possible to foster true human development without education. In this regard, the United Nations Development Program has defined three criteria for human development since its first report in 1990: education, health, and income.[2]

There is also the concept of human capital which indicates that people, like other resources in any given society, are the real capital; therefore, investing in them

---

1 Jamal Sanad Al-Suwaidi, *United Arab Emirates Society: A Future Perspective* [in Arabic], Emirates Lectures Series, no. 71 (Abu Dhabi: Emirates Center for Strategic Studies and Research, 2003), p. 39.

2 Faisal Ahmad Buteebah, *Return on Investment in Education* [in Arabic] (Amman: Dar Al-Yazouri for Publishing and Distribution, 2013), p. 22.

through education is an investment that aims to ensure development in its comprehensive sense,[1] on the grounds of progress in the fields of production, industry, and technology, among others. It is linked to the human knowledge base in society. Also, global powers are no longer fighting over material resources, rather over knowledge,[2] which indicates that only societies that invest in human capital by providing the appropriate education, training, and qualification, can withstand such a fight.

In this regard, Klaus Schwab, founder and executive chairman of the World Economic Forum, stressed, during his participation in a session at the World Government Summit 2016 in Dubai, that world governments should focus on three aspects if they want to keep pace with the Fourth Industrial Revolution (4IR) and its massive underlying changes: developing human capital, fostering innovation and creativity, and providing a decent life for their people.[3]

---

1 Sa'doun Hmoud Al-Rbei'awi and Hussein Waleed Abbas, *Intellectual Capital* [in Arabic] (Amman: Dar Ghaida' Publishing and Distribution, 2015), p. 83.

2 Mohammad Mousawi, "Investment in Human Capital and Its Effect on Economic Growth: Case of Algeria 1970-2011" [in Arabic], PhD Diss., Faculty of Economic Sciences, Management and Commercial Sciences, University of Abou Bakr Belkaïd, Tlemcen (Algeria), 2015, pp. 32-33.

3 Abdullatif Al-Shamsi, "Vision 2.0: Together Toward the UAE Centennial," [in Arabic], in *Education and Development: Investing in the Future* (Abu Dhabi: Emirates Center for Strategic Studies and Research, 2017), p. 52.

Traditional economic thought maintained that growth is measured according to accumulated material wealth, and that material capital is the criterion of development. However, this perception has changed, and the interest in human capital is increasing significantly, since this capital is one of the key aspects of development in all societies.[1] Therefore, investing in the promotion of human development through education, health, training, and qualification has become closely related to development in its global sense. The development of human capital is no longer perceived as a financial burden that governments must shoulder, but as an investment that triggers tangible returns.[2] Some studies emphasize that "investment in human capital, rather than in machines, would have a greater impact on growth."[3]

Precise statistics included in specialized studies prove that investment in people to build human capital is a productive investment that generates real returns. For example, The Changing Wealth of Nations 2018 report,

---

1 Abdulkareem Ahmad Jameel, *Modern Human Development* [in Arabic] (Amman: Dar Al Janadriyyah for Publishing and Distribution, 2017), pp.7-8.

2 Sa'doun Hmoud Al-Rbei'awi and Hussein Waleed Abbas, *Intellectual Capital* [in Arabic] (Amman: Dar Ghaida' Publishing and Distribution, 2015), pp. 83-84.

3 Faisal Ahmad Buteebah, *Return on Investment in Education* [in Arabic] (Amman: Dar Al-Yazouri for Publishing and Distribution, 2013), p. 16.

published by the World Bank Group on January 30, 2018,[1] emphasizes that human capital constitutes a major part of wealth in high-income economies, while natural capital (including minerals, forests, and all other natural resources) accounted for 50 percent of the overall national wealth in low-income countries from 1995 to 2014.[2] The report adds that strengthening and investing in human capital helps countries worldwide to increase their national wealth and consolidate their economic growth.[3]

Other estimations by the World Bank Group show that completing another year of school can increase a person's earnings by 10 percent a year.[4] This is typically more than what any other investment could trigger, such as treasury bills, treasury bonds, and savings accounts. Also, the value of human capital – the share of human capital in total wealth – is 62 percent.[5] Moreover, 64 percent of growth in 192 countries worldwide is generated by human capital, 20

---

1   See: Glenn-Marie Lange, Quentin Wodon, and Kevin Carey eds. *The Changing Wealth of Nations 2018: Building a Sustainable Future.* Washington, DC: International Bank for Reconstruction and Development / The World Bank, 2018. https://bit.ly/2EnkWdu

2   Ibid.

3   Ibid.

4   Harry A. Patrinos, "Why education matters for economic development," World Bank blogs, May 17, 2016, http://blogs.worldbank.org/education/why-education-matters-economic-development

5   Ibid.

percent by natural capital, and 16 percent by machines, equipment, infrastructure, and other material aspects.[1]

Studies indicate that 90 percent of the growth in industrial countries in the 1960s was linked to the improvement of people's capabilities and skills, in addition to knowledge and management.[2] Furthermore, human capital is distinguished by its productivity, which increases correspondingly as people gain more expertise and improve their skills, while it is not affected by the decrease of marginal utility.[3]

The UAE devotes considerable attention to the development of human capital and the building up of national cadres, as the late Sheikh Zayed (may God rest his soul in peace) believed that, "The true wealth lies in men, and not in money or oil. Money is not useful if it is not dedicated to serving the people."[4] He also said, "No matter how many buildings, foundations, schools, and

---

1   Abdullah Al-Raisi, "The Development Dimension of Education in the UAE" [in Arabic], in *Education and Development: Investing in the Future* (Abu Dhabi: Emirates Center for Strategic Studies and Research, 2017), p. 31.

2   Mohammad Mousawi, "Investment in Human Capital and Its Effect on Economic Growth: Case of Algeria 1970-2011" [in Arabic], PhD Diss., Faculty of Economic Sciences, Management and Commercial Sciences, University of Abou Bakr Belkaïd, Tlemcen (Algeria), 2015, p. 45.

3   Ibid. p. 39.

4   Salman Kassed, "Zayed and the UAE: Reading into the Personality of the Nation Builder and the Philosophy of Nation Building" [in Arabic], *Al-Ittihad* (Abu Dhabi), July 30, 2009.

hospitals we build, or how many bridges we raise, all these are material entities. The real spirit behind the progress is the human spirit, the able man with his intellect and capabilities."[1]

His Highness Sheikh Khalifa bin Zayed Al Nahyan, President of the UAE (may God protect him), has adopted the same approach, constantly emphasizing that people are at the center of development.[2] His Highness Sheikh Mohammed bin Rashid Al Maktoum, Vice President and Prime Minister of the UAE and Ruler of Dubai (may God protect him),[3] and His Highness Sheikh Mohamed bin Zayed Al Nahyan, Crown Prince of Abu Dhabi and Deputy Supreme Commander of the UAE Armed Forces (may God protect him),[4] also follow the same path and emphasize the same interest in the various development plans in the UAE, especially those that are future-oriented.[5]

---

1 Yousef Mohammad Al-Madfa'i, *Zayed and the UAE: Building the Union State* [in Arabic] (Abu Dhabi: Abu Dhabi Authority for Culture and Heritage, 2008), p. 190.

2 "Khalifa Puts Human Development and Empowerment of Citizens at the Forefront of the Priorities of the National Strategies for Action" [in Arabic], *Al Khaleej* (Sharjah), June 22, 2013.

3 "Mohammed bin Rashid honors second group of diploma in government innovation course," Emirates News Agency, February 4, 2018, http://wam.ae/en/details/1395302664769

4 "Abu Dhabi Crown Prince receives delegation from ACTVET," Emirates News Agency, November 14, 2017, http://wam.ae/en/details/1395302646561

5 For example, UAE Vision 2021, UAE Centennial 2071, Abu Dhabi Economic Vision 2030, and others. In all these plans, the human development of UAE nationals is a central matter as they are seen as the true wealth of the country.

In 2015, the Federal Authority for Government Human Resources[1] inaugurated a world center for human resources development, seeking to elaborate strategies and solutions to address challenges facing human resources.[2] Consequently, the UAE topped the rank in the Arab world and in the region according to the Global Human Capital Index, issued by the World Economic Forum on September 12, 2017.[3]

Despite the considerable efforts that have been exerted in order to build local human capabilities, primarily in light of the UAE leadership's awareness of the pivotal role of the human component in preparation for the post-oil era, there are still numerous questions that need to be raised in the framework of the strategy to prepare local human resources. Here are five of these questions:

- Are the adopted policies, strategies, and plans to prepare and build human cadres keeping pace with the accelerating developments around the world, or do they need to be revised?

---

1 See: UAE Federal Authority for Government Human Resources, https://www.fahr.gov.ae.

2 "UAE launches world-class center for human resources development," [in Arabic], *Al-Ittihad* (Abu Dhabi), April 20, 2015.

3 See: *The Global Human Capital Report 2017*, World Economic Forum, https://bit.ly/2wq8Vz6

- What are the possible ways to prepare and qualify the Emirati human cadres that graduated from universities many years ago, or those that have already joined the labor market, in order to cope with the requirements of future jobs as well as with the emerging changes in the job market in general?

- Are the UAE's education institutions providing the necessary attention to the studies and reports that address the major changes in the nature of jobs, the labor market, and the necessary skills of the future? Are these institutions on the right path to appropriately developing their curricula and mechanisms?

- Is the private sector in the UAE aware of its role in this regard, or is it still far from the desired real partnership with education institutions, in order to match education outputs with labor market needs?

- Is the human base in the UAE aware of the changes in the labor market and its future requirements, which necessitate the changing of culture, priorities, and choices, mainly in the age of technology?

The importance of the previous question stems from the fact that, according to an opinion poll conducted by the Emirates Center for Strategic Studies and Research in 2018, the majority of UAE citizens would prefer to take up government or military jobs (72.9 percent), and 56.7 percent think that they will remain in the same field throughout their professional career.[1]

These results show that there is a problem in societal awareness regarding the actual and future global changes, as it is expected that "65 percent of children in primary school will grow up to work in jobs that do not exist today...[and] 47 percent of job categories are at high risk of ceasing to exist because they can be automated."[2]

---

1 Emirates Center for Strategic Studies and Research, "Position of the UAE citizens on the education system and the job market," unpublished poll, 2018.

2 Sheikh Mohammed bin Rashid Al Maktoum, "Governments must be engines of innovation," *The National*, February 4, 2015, https://bit.ly/2oc Qj3W.

5

National Identity: Significance and Sources of Threats

"Your country is waiting for you to contribute to the Union process. We have to work together for its good, its security, and its stability."

Zayed bin Sultan Al Nahyan

I n any society, identity represents a critical issue because it defines how society views itself and how it views others.[1] Globalization has transformed the world into a single small village. It has led to the weakening or disappearance of boundaries and restrictions that were once imposed on the flow of people, cultures, and ideas across the world.[2] Hence, the identity issue has become a vast plight that not only plagues developing countries, which harbor deep concerns about losing their identity in favor of outside influences (European and American),[3] but also in the Western countries themselves—first of all the US. This is what prompted the renowned American thinker, the late Samuel Huntington, to dedicate his 2004 book, titled *Who Are We? The Challenges to America's National Identity*,[4] to exploring the threats that American identity faces. He came to the conclusion that the greatest of these threats emanates from Latin minorities, in particular the Mexicans.

---

1 For more details see, Anthony D. Smith, *National Identity* (Las Vegas: University of Nevada Press, 1991).

2 Hussein Ali Ibrahim Al-Falahi, *New Globalization: Dimensions and Repercussions* [in Arabic] (Amman: Dar Ghaida' Publishing and Distribution, 2014), p. 38. See also: Rashid Abbas Al-Jazrawi, *The Phenomenon of Globalization and Its Impact on Unemployment in the Arab World* [in Arabic] (Amman: Academic Book Center, 2015), p. 15.

3 For more details see, Fahad Mishary Al-Dhafiri, *Globalization and National Identity* [in Arabic], (Kuwait: Dar Qurtas Publishing, 2002). See also: Ayoub Dakhlallah, *Education and the Problems of Society in an Era of Globalization* [in Arabic] (Beirut: Dar al-Kotob Al-Ilmiyah, 2015), p. 112.

4 Samuel P. Huntington, *Who Are We? The Challenges to America's National Identity*, (London: The Free Press, 2004).

Many people believe that the US presidential election of 2016, which brought Donald Trump to power, reflected in one of its aspects a crisis in the American identity.[1] However, the identity issue is not only limited to the US. Several European countries began to examine with concern the identity issue caused by the growing flow of immigration and the increasing number of Muslims, which have triggered waves of "Islamophobia" in their societies.[2] The position of many European countries toward migrants from the Arab and Islamic countries mirrors their fear about losing their cultural and civilizational identity.[3]

The study *United Arab Emirates Society: A Future Perspective*[4] underestimated the scale and magnitude of the implications of globalization on UAE national identity, in particular, and that of the GCC countries, in general. That underestimation was based on inherent structural factors in the Arab-Islamic composition that make the people in the

---

1 Strategic Fiker Center for Studies, "The future of Arab- U.S. relations after Trump's victory: an assessment of a position" [in Arabic], 2016, p. 4, https://bit.ly/2ut6A8c

2 Rabeh Zaghouni, "Islamophobia and the rise of the extreme right in Europe: a socio-cultural approach" [in Arabic], *Al Mustaqbal Al-Arabi*, no. 421 (Beirut: Centre for Arab Unity Studies, March, 2014).

3 Hani Suleiman, "European policies toward refugees: the tripartite of security, identity, and human values" [in Arabic] (Cairo: Arab Center for Research and Studies, August 29, 2016): http://www.acrseg.org/40345.

4 Jamal Sanad Al-Suwaidi, *United Arab Emirates Society: A Future Perspective* [in Arabic], Emirates Lectures Series, no. 71 (Abu Dhabi: Emirates Center for Strategic Studies and Research. 2003).

region highly adaptable to the requirements of change and modernization, and at the same time, able to preserve the genuine values, heritage, and traditions that make up their identity.[1]

Today, when I examine the issue after a decade and a half since the release of this study, and review it in light of new indicators and great transformations that have beset the region over the past years, I find that the Emirati and Arab identities are experiencing a real and serious threat. When the study was first published in 2003, this threat was not as apparent or as acute as it is today. There are many reasons for this:

First, the communications and information revolution in 2003 was not as deep, immense, influential, and fast-moving as it is today, and the Arab people, especially the youth, were not so exposed to it. Today, it poses a clear threat to culture, values, customs, traditions, and identity. The first statistical survey in 1996 showed that there were about 40 million Internet users worldwide.[2] Another survey, conducted in 2013, showed that the number of Internet users had increased to 2.5 billion worldwide.[3]

---

1 Jamal Sanad Al-Suwaidi, *United Arab Emirates Society: A Future Perspective* [in Arabic], Emirates Lectures Series, no. 71 (Abu Dhabi: Emirates Center for Strategic Studies and Research, 2003), p. 20.

2 Sangin Park, *Strategies and Policies in Digital Convergence,* (Hershey: Idea Group Reference, 2007), p. x.

3 "Internet Growth Statistics 1995 to 2017—The Global Village Online," Internet World Stats, https://www.internetworldstats.com/emarketing.htm

According to the United Nations statistics, this number had reached 3.2 billion by the end of 2015[1] and 3.5 billion in 2016. This represents 47 percent of the earth's population.[2] In 2017, there were 3.6 billion Internet users.[3] An August 2017 report by the United States International Trade Commission indicated a 12-fold volume increase in the information flow via the Internet between 2007 and 2016,[4] as illustrated in Table 5-1, below.

Table 5-1

Number of Internet Users in the World (1996-2017)

Year	No. of Internet Users
1996	40 Million
2013	2.5 Billion
2015	3.2 Billion
2016	3.5 Billion
2017	3.6 Billion

Source: "Internet Growth Statistics 1995 to 2017—The Global Village Online," Internet World Stats.

---

1 "Internet users reached 3.2 billion in 2015" [in Arabic], *Al Sharq Al-Awsat* (London), February 23, 2016.

2 "Half of the Earth's population would use the Internet by the end of 2016" [in Arabic], *Al-Ittihad* (Abu Dhabi), November 23, 2016.

3 Statista, The Statistics Portal, https://www.statista.com/statistics/273018/number-of-internet-users-worldwide/

4 United States International Trade Commission, "Global Digital Trade 1: Market Opportunities and Key Foreign Trade Restrictions," USITC Publication 4716, August 2017.

This has caused explicit and implicit effects on the national identity of different countries because, as the Arab thinker Galal Amin used to say,[1] "Globalization always bears some sort of cultural invasion; in another sense, the stronger culture subdues the weaker one,"[2] and the ability of the more technologically advanced cultures and civilizations is to penetrate less advanced cultures and societies.[3]

According to Amro Salah, modern technology, along with communications and information technology, has created a national identity that is geographically un-bound to the homeland, has promoted foreign shared values over home shared values of citizens in different countries, has enhanced the values of globalization in face of the values of national identity, and has provided an alternative platform in the virtual space for the individual in countries that deny their citizens such a platform in reality.[4] Additionally, the modern communications revolution has abolished the geo-graphical space as a collective pot for identity, which

---

1   Galal Amin, *Globalization* [in Arabic] (Cairo, Dar Al-Shorouq, 2001), p. 48.

2   Ibid. p. 48.

3   Khalil Nouri Al-Aani, *Islamic Identity in the Age of Cultural Globalization* [in Arabic] (Baghdad: Sunni Endowment Diwan, 2009), p. 128.

4   Amro Salah, "Modern nationalism: building identity in technological societies: Singapore as a model" [in Arabic] (Abu Dhabi: Future for Advanced Research and Studies (FARAS), January 16, 2017), https://bit.ly/2HsMTD0.

weakened the sense of national affiliation among different nations.[1]

Second, if the communication revolution represents a common danger in the Arab region, this danger is then more acute in societies that are more exposed to this revolution such as the UAE, which ranks first in the Middle East region with regards to the number of Internet users compared to the total population number with 71 percent, according to the "Serviceplan Middle East" report 2014.[2]

Official data in 2017 indicated that 90 percent of the UAE population have access to the Internet, which is considered one of the highest access rates in the world. The UAE ranked first in the world in terms of Smartphone usage compared to the total population, according to what the Director General of the UAE Telecommunications Regulatory Authority (TRA) said at a specialized conference in 2017.[3]

---

1   See: Mustafa Awfi and Zainab Omrani, "National identity in light of modern information and communications technology" [in Arabic], *Ilum Al-Insan wa Al-Mujtamaa*, no. 4, (Algeria: University Mohamed Khider of Biskra, December 2012), pp 15-45.

2   "UAE tops the region in the number of Internet users" [in Arabic], *Al Bayan* (Dubai), April 28, 2014.

3   "90 percent of UAE population have access to the Internet" [in Arabic], *Al-Ittihad* (Abu Dhabi), October 31, 2017.

According to a McKinsey report in October 2016, the UAE leads the Middle East region in digital technology;[1] furthermore, it has achieved the first place regionally and the 18th rank globally as one of the most competitive countries in the "IMD World Digital Competitiveness Ranking 2017," issued by the World Competitiveness Center of the Institute for Management Development in Switzerland.[2]

Third, nowadays, the Arab region is witnessing sectarian, doctrinal, and ethnic conflicts that have never been so intense throughout the region's modern history. Those religious, ethnic, or sectarian conflicts pose the most dangerous threat to national identity.[3]

This trend will apparently escalate in the region in the coming years as a result of multiple factors such as: the existing political conflicts and the rising separatist aspirations of some ethnic, religious, or doctrinal

---

1 Tarek Elmasry, Enrico Benni, Jigar Patel, Jan Peter and Dem Moore, "Digital Middle East: Transforming the region into a leading digital economy," McKinsey, October 2016, https://bit.ly/2EJRgHA

2 IMD World Competitiveness Center, "IMD World Digital Competitiveness Ranking 2017," https://bit.ly/2D7TCQt

3 Ahmed Yousef Ahmed et al., *Future of Change in the Arab World* [in Arabic] (Beirut: Center for Arab Unity Studies, 2016), p. 56. See also: Salah al-Mukhtar, *America's Syndrome: Is it an Arab Spring or the Second Sykes-Picot?* [in Arabic] (London: E-Book Ltd., 2016), p. 19.

minorities in the region,[1] since there are some foreign schemes that seek to destabilize the region on an ethnic, sectarian, doctrinal, and religious basis.[2] Undoubtedly, the most serious danger that can threaten the national identity of any nation or country is the spread of sectarian, doctrinal, and ethnic tendencies at the expense of the collective national identity.

Fourth, the powers of political Islam, spearheaded by the Muslim Brotherhood,[3] pose a serious challenge to the national identity in the Arab region. Because this group does not recognize identity, as it favors another transnational identity based on the concepts of the Islamic Caliphate and Umma (nation) and other outdated concepts[4], the Muslim Brotherhood represents the greatest threat to national identity. It takes a hostile position on history, heritage, culture, customs,

---

1   Saad Eddin Ibrahim, *On the Issue of Unity and the Decline of Pan-Arabism* [in Arabic] (Cairo: Dar Ibn Roshd, 2018), p. 22.

2   Jassem Al-Hariri, *Israeli Schemes to Dismantle the Arab Region: Iraq 1948-2013, A Case Study* [in Arabic] (Amman: Dar Al-Jenan Books, 2014). See also: Mustafa Ahmed, *The Global Conspiracy. Fourth Generation Warfare: The Modern Application of The Protocols of the Elders of Zion* [in Arabic] (Cairo: El-Sherif Mass Publication and Distribution, 2017), p. 70.

3   For more details about the Muslim Brotherhood and its ideas see: Jamal Sanad Al-Suwaidi, *The Mirage* (Abu Dhabi, 2015), pp. 259-362.

4   Jamal Sanad Al-Suwaidi, *Events That Changed History* [in Arabic] (Abu Dhabi, 2018), pp. 93-102.

and traditions that are incompatible with the group's own interpretation of religion.[1]

Fifth, the Arabic language that has preserved the Arab and Islamic identity against the colonial tide in the region over centuries is under serious threat from foreign languages. UNESCO predicts that 90 percent of current languages will be replaced by other languages by the end of the 21st century,[2] while 234 indigenous languages completely disappeared during the 20th century.[3] This is cause for deep concern as our Arabic language is no longer immune to this danger. This danger is aggravated by the weak state of scientific and

---

1 Mohamed Hussein Abul-Ela, *Religious Violence in Egypt: A Reading in Islamic Thought* [in Arabic] (Cairo: Mahrousa Center for Publishing, Press Services and Information, 2007), p. 236.

2 The document "Language Vitality and Endangerment" [in Arabic] states that, "About 97 percent of the world's people speak about 4 percent of the world's languages; conversely, about 96 percent of the world's languages are spoken by about 3 percent of the world's people. Even languages with many thousands of speakers are no longer being acquired by children; at least 50 percent of the more than six thousand languages in the world are losing speakers." See: the International Expert Meeting on UNESCO Program Safeguarding of Endangered Languages, p.4, UNESCO website, http://www.unesco.org/new/fileadmin/MULTIMEDIA/HQ/CLT/pdf/Language_vitality_and_endangerment_AR.pdf.

3 Ali Nasser Kenana, *Culture and Its Manifestations: Surface and Depth* [in Arabic] (Beirut: *Al Rihab Publisher* Est., 2016), p. 19.

intellectual production in the Arabic language.[1]
Statistics reveal that one book is issued for every 12,000
Arab citizens compared to one book for every 500
British citizens or 900 German citizens.[2] The number
of books that are translated into Arabic does not
exceed 330 titles per year, which is a fifth of what is
being translated into Greek, for example. The number
of Arabic books that have been translated from other
languages since the reign of the Abbasid Caliph Al-
Mamun[3] (786-833 AD) until now is no more than
100,000 titles, which equals the amount of books that
Spain translates into Spanish in just one year.[4] This is
one of the factors that contribute to the marginalization
of Arabic, as well as the immigration of Arabic native
speakers to other languages in order to keep in touch
with modern thought, science, and technology in the

---

1 Hassib Abdel Halim Shoaib, *A Teacher's Reference in the Teaching Methods of
   Arabic Language in the Primary, Middle, and Secondary School Levels* [in Arabic]
   (Beirut: Dar al-Kotob Al-Ilmiyah, 2015), p. 28.

2 Rawa Zaki Al-Taweel, *Sustainable Development in Light of Democracy and
   Human Rights* [in Arabic] (Amman: Zahran Publishers, 2009), p. 271.

3 Abū Al-Abbās Abdullah Al-ma'mūn Ibn Harun Al-Rashid, (born 786,
   Baghdad—died 833, Tarsus). He was the seventh Abbasid Caliph. For more
   details, https://www.britannica.com/biography/al-Mamun.

4 Fatima Ahmed Al Khazaleh, *Communications and Education Technology* [in
   Arabic] (Amman: Dar Al-Majd Publishing and Distribution, 2014), p. 94.

world. Another factor is the very weak Arabic content that exists on the Internet.[1]

Sixth, one of the most important threats to identity is that some scholars have adopted distorted concepts in regard to modernity and its correlation to identity in Arab and Islamic societies. Some scholars place modernity in complete contradiction with the culture, heritage, history, and identity of society while others believe that preserving identity impedes modernity and progress.[2]

Finally, the exacerbating demographic imbalance in the UAE over the past decades has had an obvious negative impact on national identity, especially on the level of language, culture, customs, and lifestyle in general. Although I have explored the different aspects, indicators, and implications of these issues, in particular on identity, in the study *United Arab Emirates Society: A Future Perspective,*[3] this imbalance has been further exacerbated in the subsequent years since the first

---

1 Rami Aboud, *The Arabic Digital Content on the Internet* [in Arabic] (Cairo: Al Arabi Publishing and Distributing, 2013).

2 Mohamed Said Bani Ayesh, *Modernity from an Islamic Perspective* [in Arabic] (Irbid: Dar Al-Kitab Al-Thaqafi, 2016), pp. 104-105.

3 Jamal Sanad Al-Suwaidi, *United Arab Emirates Society: A Future Perspective* [in Arabic], Emirates Lectures Series, no. 71 (Abu Dhabi: Emirates Center for Strategic Studies and Research, 2003), pp. 39-47.

edition of the study was published in 2003. The ratio of Emiratis to expatriates in the UAE was 25 percent in 2001,[1] but this percentage fell to 12 percent, as per the 2015 statistics,[2] and reached 11.48 percent in 2018, according to other estimates.[3] There is no doubt that such a trend would increase the negative impact of the demographic imbalance on national identity.

Within the aforementioned context, it can be said that identity is not just a mere socio-cultural concept; rather it lies at the core of the national security system of any society. Societies that lose their identity become vulnerable to infiltration and threats. Identity works as a safety mechanism for society because it binds society with its heritage, customs, tradition, and values and serves as a bridge between the past, present, and the future.[4]

---

1 Jamal Sanad Al-Suwaidi, *United Arab Emirates Society: A Future Perspective* [in Arabic], Emirates Lectures Series, no. 71 (Abu Dhabi: Emirates Center for Strategic Studies and Research, 2003), p. 39.

2 "CIA World Fact book, United Arab Emirates" https://www.cia.gov/library/publications/the-world-factbook/geos/ae.html.

3 "United Arab Emirates Population Statistics (2018)," https://bit.ly/2mm4y5B.

4 For more details about the correlation between identity and national identity, see: Faten Mohammed Razak and Alaa Jabbar Ahmed, "The weakness of the national identity and its implication on the Iraqi national security" [in Arabic], *Asiyasiat wa Al-Duwalia* (Baghdad: University of Mustansiriyah, 2015), pp. 453-488.

Furthermore, identity is a political concept that is associated with citizenship. Countries lacking a collective political identity suffer from the emergence of ethnic, tribal, regional, religious, and doctrinal sub-identities. Such situations constitute the most serious danger to the stability, security, and very existence of societies. The most meaningful words in this regard are expressed by His Highness Sheikh Khalifa bin Zayed Al Nahyan, President of the UAE (may God protect him), when he said, "He, who does not have identity, does not exist in the present, and has no place in the future."[1]

However, a question arises: does preserving identity imply stagnation, arrested development, rejection of modernity, and clinging to the past at the expense of the present and the future? Unfortunately, there are some people who adopt and hold to this vision and view everything from beyond the border – both ideas or culture – as an absolute source of threat and danger to our identity.[2] Indeed, some powers in the world view their culture, ideas, visions, and orientations as better and more noble and want, therefore, to impose them on other nations.

---

1   "Khalifa: historical leadership and approach to national action" [in Arabic], *Al Bayan* (Dubai), June 30, 2013.

2   Mohamed Said Bani Ayesh, *Modernity from an Islamic Perspective* [in Arabic] (Irbid: Dar Al-Kitab Al-Thaqafi, 2016), p. 104.

Francis Fukuyama's thesis, *The End of History and the Last Man*,[1] was not just of a political-economic dimension, but it also had a cultural dimension. It implied the final victory of the Western capitalist model with its political, economic, cultural, and social aspects.[2] Despite all that, dealing with the issue of identity, whether in the UAE or the rest of the Arab and Islamic countries, should be governed by a number of basic considerations:

First, excluding others' languages and cultures is not the appropriate way to preserve one's identity. Rather, it leads to stagnation and isolationism. The solution, as I see it, lies in the wonderful quote of the iconic Indian leader Mahatma Gandhi, who said, "I do not want my house to be walled in on all sides and my windows to be stuffed. I want the culture of all lands to be blown about my house as freely as possible. But I refuse to be blown off my feet by any."[3]

Second, preserving one's own identity does not negate progress, modernity, or openness to the world; both ends can be achieved simultaneously. Lessons can

---

1 Francis Fukuyama, *The End of History and the Last Man* (USA: Free Press, 1992).

2 Ibid.

3 Dia Kohl, "Winds of cultures and preserving heritage" [in Arabic], *Al Khaleej* (Sharjah) September 1, 2014.

be drawn from the experience of several countries, especially that of Japan,[1] Singapore,[2] and South Korea.[3] These countries embraced modern science to develop themselves until they reached the rank of developed countries. At the same time, they succeeded in maintaining their cultural and civilizational identities.

Third, identity is an evolving concept, in the sense that it does not refer to a stalemate or clinging to the past, but it is important to redefine our identity by mixing between the past and the present and coupling the old with the modern. Emirati identity should not be limited to heritage, language, history, customs, and traditions. It is important to create a modern concept of identity that accommodates the developments that took place within Emirati society and in the regional and international arena. Along with history, language, and heritage, this concept should also include tolerance, acceptance of the other, unity, sacrifice, standing up for truth and righteousness, and openness to the world. This is key where there are

---

1 Younis Muayad Younis, *The Roles of the Great Asian Powers in the Strategic Balance in Asia after the Cold War and Their Future Prospects* [in Arabic] (Amman: Academic for Publishing & Distributing), p. 92.

2 Amro Salah, "Modern nationalism: building identity in technological societies: Singapore as a model" [in Arabic] (Abu Dhabi: Future for Advanced Research and Studies (FARAS), January 16, 2017), https://bit.ly/2HsMTD0.

3 Saad bin Nasir Al-Hussein, "The Korean experiment: from the developing world to the first world" [in Arabic], *Al-Riyadh* (Riyadh) January 11, 2011.

several changes that have direct effects on the national identity; the most important of which are these two changes:

1. The UAE's participation in the operation to restore legitimacy in Yemen where some of the UAE's servicemen have fallen as martyrs. This has introduced the Emirati identity to new concepts such as martyrdom in the sake of righteousness and truth, and readiness to fight abroad to defend national and Arab security, as well as the brotherly countries'.[1]

2. The UAE National Service Law has reinforced national identity by promoting the values of patriotism, belonging, loyalty, and sacrifice for the sake of the homeland.[2]

Fourth, identity is not just a formal issue that is associated with customs, traditions, or national and religious occasions; instead, it is an intrinsic issue of values, in the sense that there is a strong bond with our original ethical values so that they are not eroded or threatened by exposure to other foreign cultures.

---

1 Maryam Butti, Ilke Denizli, and Tarik Chelali, "The Martyr and the Nation: The UAE, Turkey, and Algeria," Delma Institute, May 22, 2018, http://drafts.delma.io/en/the-martyr-and-the-nation-the-uae-turkey-and-algeria

2 For more details about the role of the UAE National Service Law in enhancing the national identity, see: Major General Staff Pilot Rashad Mohamed Salem Al-Saadi, *The National Service and Its Security, Military, and Development Effects in the UAE* [in Arabic] (Abu Dhabi, 2015), pp. 30-31. See also: "UAE National Service Law and promotion of identity" [in Arabic], *Nation Shield* (Abu Dhabi, 2014).

Fifth, the global intercultural relationship should not be of a confrontational nature, rather a relationship of interaction. It should not be a zero-sum relationship whereby each culture seeks to replace, marginalize, and defeat the other, because the diversity of cultures and identities represents a source of enrichment to the world.

6

Balanced Political Development: Recipe for UAE Stability

"Members of the Federal National Council are all sons and brothers who should be relied on and consulted. They shoulder a heavy responsibility toward the nation and the homeland. They should pay attention to every small detail, and collaborate for the best, in order to become the watchful eyes that take care of their brothers and sons, and be the foremost guards and protectors against any potential threat."

Zayed bin Sultan Al Nahyan

I n addressing the political aspect of the comprehensive development vision for UAE society in the study titled *United Arab Emirates Society: A Future Perspective*,[1] I was careful to use the concept of "political development,"[2] instead of the concept of "political reform,"[3] "political

---

1 Jamal Sanad Al-Suwaidi, *United Arab Emirates Society: A Future* Perspective [in Arabic], Emirates Lectures Series, no. 71 (Abu Dhabi: Emirates Center for Strategic Studies and Research. 2003).

2 There are different definitions of the concept of political development; however, there is consensus among political and social scholars that this concept entails three aspects or elements: first, equality within society and equality before the law; second, the so-called political capability, in the sense of the effective ability of the political system to achieve and deliver. This includes accountability, transparency, and sound management; third, specialization. Each component of the political system has its own specific functions without overlapping of functions. See: Thamer Kamel Mohammed Al-Khazraji, *Modern Political Systems and Public Policies: A Contemporary Study of the Power Management Strategy* [in Arabic] (Amman: Majdalawi for Publishing and Distribution, 2004), pp. 140-141. For more details on the concept of political development, see: Saleh Belhaj, "Political development: view of concepts and theories" [in Arabic], Algeria, Hassiba Benbouali University of Chlef website, https://bit.ly/2K8KGkK

3 Arabi defines political reform as "the sum of operations that take place at the level of the political system with the aim of gradual adjustment of laws, legislations, institutions, structures, frameworks, mechanisms, performance, behaviors, and prevailing political culture in order to cope with changes in the internal and external environment, responding to the challenges facing the system in a way that guarantees citizens more political participation, ensures the effectiveness and efficiency of the state institutions, and stresses the protection of the basic freedoms and rights." See: Muslim Baba Arabi, "An Attempt to explore the concept of political reform" [in Arabic], *Cahiers de Politique & de Droit* no. 9, (Algiers: Université Kasdi Merbah Ouargla, June 2013), p. 241.

modernization,"[1] "democracy," or any other notion that conveys the same meaning. My rationale behind this choice was that the concept of political development is broader and more comprehensive, which the UAE and Arab societies needed, in seeking a real modernization process that focuses more on the essence and content than on the form, and prioritizes values and purposes over procedures.

The concept of political development puts an emphasis on numerous and overlapping aspects: political, social, cultural, legal, economic, and administrative, among others. It focuses on citizenship, equality, political and administrative efficiency, participation in public affairs, enhancement of the role of women, institutionalism, political and social stability, justice, accountability, transparency, governance, as well as other values and concepts that consist of the preconditions to ensure a real political development of any society.[2]

In this context, the concept of political development is closer to the concept of good governance, which is

---

1 The term political modernization implies: industrialization and technological advancement, establishing stable and effective institutions, and separation of state and religion through secularism. The concept is specifically associated with the Renaissance in Europe. See: Muslim Baba Arabi, "An Attempt to explore the concept of political reform" [in Arabic], *Cahiers de Politique & de Droit* no. 9, (Algiers: Université Kasdi Merbah Ouargla, June 2013), p. 242.

2 For more details on elements or components of this concept, see: Thamer Kamel Mohammed Al-Khazraji, *Modern Political Systems and Public Policies: A Contemporary Study of the Power Management Strategy* [in Arabic] (Amman: Majdalawi for Publishing and Distribution, 2004), pp. 133- 157.

considered one of the fundamental concepts used to discuss the quality of governance. It encompasses several key aspects, mainly transparency, accountability, participation, justice, the rule of law, efficiency, effectiveness,[1] strategic vision, decentralization, equality, and consensus.[2]

On this basis, the study *United Arab Emirates Society: A Future Perspective* sheds light on a number of necessary aspects for political development in the UAE, mainly:[3]

- Continuing the transition process toward an institutional life, which is assigned the responsibility of reviewing public policies, and ensuring all citizens contribute to the management and development of their society.

- Seeking to come up with a system based on administrative accountability and public policy monitoring.

- Overcoming centralized bureaucracy and hierarchical administration, and focusing on decentralized structures, in order to ensure optimal efficiency in responding to people's needs and ability to provide better services.

---

1 Salem Dalah, "From the rule of law to good governance: integration of basis, mechanisms, and objective" [in Arabic], *Damascus University Journal for the Economic and Legal Sciences*, vol. 30, no.2 (2014), pp. 89-94.

2 Imrani Karbusa, "Good governance and the future of sustainable development in Algeria" [in Arabic] (Algiers, Hassiba Benbouali University of Chlef) https://bit.ly/2I0hGdP.

3 Jamal Sanad Al-Suwaidi, *United Arab Emirates Society: A Future Perspective* [in Arabic], Emirates Lectures Series, no. 71 (Abu Dhabi: Emirates Center for Strategic Studies and Research, 2003), pp. 24-27.

- Making the Federal National Council (FNC) a fully or partially elected council and expanding its prerogatives.

- Enhancing the political, economic, and social role of women in society and expanding their participation and contribution to the shaping of the future.

- Improving transparency and administrative accountability and making public departments more flexible and responsive to the needs of citizens.

- Seeking to instill the concept of citizenship and its links to established rights and specified obligations within society.

This vision, introduced in the study 15 years ago, provided a depiction of a real political development, not only in the UAE, but also in the GCC countries and Arab region. However, the problem that has persisted in several Arab societies, during the last few years, has been the reduction of the reform and political development process to elections and changing of governments, disregarding the cultural, social, and economic specificities of these societies,[1] which explains the negative, and sometimes critical and catastrophic, results of this process. What would be

---

1 Ibrahim Abrash, *Political Sociology: An Epistemological Approach and an Applied Study on the Arab World* [in Arabic] (London: E-Kutub Ltd., 2011), p. 193.

expected from elections in a society that suffers from poverty; ignorance; religious, ethnic, and sectarian hostilities; lack of tolerance, coexistence, citizenship, and justice; and prevalence of discrimination against women?[1] This was the case in the elections that took place in some Arab countries in the years that followed 2011, as doctrinal, ethnic, and religious conflicts prevailed, adding more to the divisions, conflicts, and instability in the societies where elections took place.[2]

Since 1971, the UAE has adopted an approach to political development featuring a wide range of characteristics. First, comprehensiveness: this means adopting an integrated vision for this development, stemming from the concept of comprehensive development that encompasses political, legal, cultural, economic, and social aspects.[3] It eventually aims to ensure stability, progress, responding to people's needs, and constantly improving their living

---

1 Political literature agrees that democracy cannot be limited to the election process because the latter is just one of the democratic measures. See: Rafik Abdel Salam, "Arab elections: misplaced priorities" [in Arabic], *Democracy* (Cairo) August 31, 2018, https://bit.ly/2LaHOU4

2 See: Hassanein Tawfiq Ibrahim, "The obstacles of democratic transformation in Arab spring countries" [in Arabic], *Democracy* (Cairo) August 31, 2014, http://democracy.ahram.org.eg/News/1045.aspx

3 On the concept of comprehensive development, see: Hamza Jabali, *Development of Human Resources Management* [in Arabic] (Amman: Dar Alam Thaqafa for Publishing & Distribution, 2016), p. 73.

standards. This approach is also in line with the concept of sustainable development that takes into account the demands and rights of both current and future generations. It considers people as the aim and the means, and accords significant importance to the development of human resources, enhancement of social participation, and preservation of cultural and civilizational specificities of society.[1]

Second, calculated progress;[2] this indicates that every step needs to be taken at the right time and in the right place, ensuring that they achieve the intended goals, because the provision of favorable conditions is an essential prerequisite for a successful development process, whether politically, socially, or economically.

Third, specificities,[3] which refers to the necessity of taking the specificities and inherent characteristics of UAE society into account, because each society is distinguished by certain features; hence, other societies' experiences can

---

1 For the meaning of sustainable development, see: Medhat Abu-Nasr and Yasmin Medhat Mohammed, *Sustainable Development: Concept, Dimensions, and Indicators* [in Arabic] (Cairo: Arab Group for Training & publishing, 2017), p. 17.

2 "The Federal National Council and the experience of political empowerment in the UAE" [in Arabic], *Nation Shield* (Abu Dhabi), August 1, 2015, https://bit.ly/2wp18GO

3 "Comprehensive development in the UAE integrates economically, socially, and politically" [in Arabic], *Al-Ittihad* (Abu Dhabi), December 25, 2014.

neither be transferred nor imitated, since they are relevant to different circumstances and environments.

Fourth, continuity, which refers to adopting the philosophy that defines development as a continuous and renewable process adapting to changing internal and external circumstances and developments.

Fifth, a citizen-oriented approach, which means considering the happiness, welfare, and stability of citizens as the ultimate goal, rather than ideologies, or political party-centered, religious, sectarian, or ethnic agendas.[1]

In my study *United Arab Emirates Society: A Future Perspective,*[2] published 15 years ago, I called for real political development in the UAE, based on enhancing citizenship, transparency, accountability, women's empowerment, enhancement of participation in public life, and government efficiency, among others. Now, I can say, with full confidence and a clear conscience, that the UAE has achieved great accomplishments along this path, and has

---

1 This was expressed by His Highness Sheikh Mohamed bin Zayed Al Nahyan, Crown Prince of Abu Dhabi and Deputy Supreme Commander of the UAE Armed Forces (may God protect him), when he said, "the UAE's main objective, since its inception, was to achieve the happiness of its citizens, promote national assets, and strengthen and consolidate the nation's position globally at all levels." [in Arabic], *Al-Ittihad* (Abu Dhabi), October 17, 2017.

2 Jamal Sanad Al-Suwaidi, *United Arab Emirates Society: A Future Perspective* [in Arabic], Emirates Lectures Series, no. 71 (Abu Dhabi: Emirates Center for Strategic Studies and Research, 2003)

become an inspiring model and a positive example for good governance, in which I would not find it hard to identify the indicators of these achievements at various levels:

- Cultural values: These values are essential for development, primarily the political development. In this context, the UAE has become a global model for coexistence, tolerance, moderation, acceptance of the other, and adoption of a humanitarian attitude toward the world. The late Sheikh Zayed bin Sultan Al Nahyan (may God rest his soul in peace) was the first to lay the foundations of tolerance in the country, and the first ruler in the region to receive a high-level award in this regard. In April 1972, Pope Paul II awarded the late Sheikh Zayed bin Sultan Al Nahyan (may God rest his soul in peace) a knighthood order, in recognition of his efforts to instill tolerance and look after the Christian community in Abu Dhabi.[1] This was also demonstrated when the UAE ranked the first regionally and third globally in the Tolerance Index of the 2016 Yearbook issued by the International Institute for Management Development in Switzerland, ahead of countries like Canada, Sweden, Netherlands, New Zealand, and Singapore.[2] This achievement did not

---

1 Mohamed El Hadi El Hanashi, *Zayed: The Pioneer of Good* [in Arabic] (Abu Dhabi: Zayed Centre for Coordination & Follow-up, July 2001), p. 42.

2 "The UAE ranks first regionally and third globally in the tolerance index" [in Arabic], *Emarat Alyoum* (Dubai), November 16, 2016.

happen arbitrarily, but as a result of a vision that has been translated into plans, strategies, and tangible projects, as manifested in the establishing of the Ministry of State for Tolerance in February 2016. His Highness Sheikh Mohammed bin Rashid Al Maktoum, Vice President and Prime Minister of the UAE and Ruler of Dubai (may God protect him), said, "We cannot allow intolerance in our country, and we cannot accept any form of discrimination against any resident or citizen."[1] In "A Message of Tolerance,"[2] published in November 2017, His Highness said, "What makes us proud of our nation is not the height of our buildings, the breadth of our streets, nor the magnitude of our shopping malls, but the openness and tolerance of our nation. Our pride stems from the fact that we are a country where everyone thrives equally, regardless of their differences, with true love and acceptance: a country where people live and work harmoniously, raising their children to enjoy a future free of the fear of

---

1 Mohammed bin Rashid Al Maktoum, *Reflections on Happiness & Positivity* [in Arabic] (Dubai: Explorer Publishing & Distribution LLC, 2017), p. 149. See also: Mohammed bin Rashid Al Maktoum, "Why ministers for happiness, tolerance, youth, and the future?" [in Arabic]: https://sheikhmohammed.ae/ar-ae/articles/details?ArticleID=710

2 A message by His Highness Sheikh Mohammed bin Rashid Al Maktoum, Vice President and Prime Minister of the UAE and Ruler of Dubai (may God protect him), to the UAE's citizens and residents in November 2017 on the occasion of the International Day for Tolerance, which takes place on November 16 of each year.

extremism, intolerance or discrimination based on their race, color, religion, sect or ethnicity."[1]

In June 2016, the UAE Cabinet approved the National Tolerance Program, in order to promote values of peace and coexistence, on the basis of Islam, the UAE Constitution, the legacy of the late Sheikh Zayed bin Sultan Al Nahyan (may God rest his soul in peace), the ethics of the UAE, international conventions, archeology and history, humanity, and common values. The program consists of numerous themes that seek to strengthen the Government's role as an incubator of tolerance, consolidate the role of family in nation building, promote tolerance among young people and prevent them from fanaticism and extremism, enrich scientific and cultural content, and integrate international efforts to promote tolerance and highlight the leading role of the UAE in this area.[2]

In July 2015, His Highness Sheikh Khalifa bin Zayed Al Nahyan, President of the UAE (may God protect him), issued a decree for Law on Combating Discrimination and Hatred Number 2 of 2015. The law

---

1 Mohammed bin Rashid Al Maktoum, *Reflections on Happiness & Positivity* [in Arabic] (Dubai: Explorer Publishing & Distribution LLC, 2017), p119.

2 For details on this program, see: "UAE Cabinet approves national tolerance program," https://bit.ly/2wtNJLp

criminalizes all acts that insult religion; eliminates all forms of discrimination; renounces hate speech through any form of expression; bans discrimination between individuals or groups on the basis of religion, belief, doctrine, sect, race, color, or ethnic origin; as well as other provisions that promote the value of tolerance in society, placing it within a strong legal framework.[1]

In 2017, the International Institute for Tolerance was launched in order to "instill the spirit of tolerance within society; build a cohesive society; promote the UAE as a role model for tolerance and anti-extremism, challenge all forms of discrimination among people on the basis of religion, gender, race, color, or language; and honor the groups or entities that contribute to the instilling of values of tolerance and dialogue between religions."[2]

This has contributed to instilling the values of tolerance and coexistence, and renouncing extremism and violence within UAE society, as amply shown in the public opinion survey conducted by the Emirates Center for Strategic Studies and Research (ECSSR) from December 10-16, 2017, on the opinion of UAE citizens about the

---

1 For more details see, "Law on Combating Discrimination and Hatred," *Federal Legislations Series*, (Abu Dhabi: Judicial Department, 2016), https://bit.ly/2I0IyKO

2 "Mohammed bin Rashid issues law on establishing international institute for tolerance" [in Arabic], *Emarat Alyoum* (Dubai), June 21, 2017.

Muslim Brotherhood. The survey covered all the UAE emirates and consisted of a sample of 2,084 respondents representing all segments of society, in terms of gender, education, income, and age, among others. The results indicated that 97.55 percent of the respondents have negative or very negative opinions about the Muslim Brotherhood.[1]

- The political level: Partial election systems have been adopted since 2006 to form the Federal National Council (FNC), following the empowerment program launched by His Highness Sheikh Khalifa bin Zayed Al Nahyan, President of the UAE (may God protect him), in 2005.[2] Since then, the electoral experience has undergone major changes to enhance the participation of citizens in public life. In the 2006 elections, half of the FNC members were chosen by an electoral college that represents a hundredfold of seats reserved for each emirate in the Council.[3] This number increased in 2011 to three-hundred fold.[4]

---

1 "98% of Emiratis reject Muslim Brotherhood," *Khaleej Times* (Dubai), January 14, 2018.

2 "Parliamentary life in the UAE" [in Arabic], UAE Ministry of State for Federal National Council Affairs, https://bit.ly/2IqKVG4

3 Wassim Husam Al-Din Al-Ahmad, *Women's and Children's Rights in light of the Gulf Legislation and Regulations* [in Arabic] (Riyadh: Law and Economics Library, 2015), p. 182.

4 "Federal National Council and the experience of political empowerment in the UAE" [in Arabic], *Nation Shield* (Abu Dhabi), August 1, 2015, https://bit.ly/2wp 18GO

In addition to the reform process that has remarkably expanded the FNC's prerogatives and highlighted the prominent role it plays in collaboration with the government in managing the affairs of the country, the 2008 constitutional amendments, regarding Articles 72 and 78, stipulate that the council's membership be expanded from two to four years, and the annual ordinary session last no less than seven months. Article 85 has been amended allowing the Federal Supreme Council to make its own bylaws, issued by decision of the President of the UAE and subject to the approval of the FNC. Also, Article 91 has been amended stating that the President of the UAE determines, by decision, the international treaties and conventions that must be referred to the FNC for consideration before they are approved.[1]

- Citizenship: The UAE has made significant strides to legally and socially consolidate the concept of citizenship,[2] which has strengthened political and social stability in society. This is manifested in the UAE's prominent positions (first in the Arab region, and

---

1 "Federal National Council and the experience of political empowerment in the UAE" [in Arabic], *Nation Shield* (Abu Dhabi), August 1, 2015, https://bit.ly/2wp 18GO

2 Rana Khaled, "Citizenship experiment in the UAE: belonging to the land" [in Arabic], *Al Bayan* (Dubai), October 13, 2007.

second worldwide) in safety and stability indexes, according to the World Economic Forum report of April 2017.[1]

- Women's role and participation in society: Emirati women have become key partners in all political, economic, and social spheres. They occupy major positions including that of minister, ambassador, judge, and chairperson and speaker of the FNC. They have become a role model to follow regionally and globally, in terms of participation and empowerment. There are nine ministers in the government, following the government reshuffle in 2017,[2] and nine members of the FNC, accounting for 22.5 percent of the FNC members.[3] According to the Global Gender Gap report, published by the World Economic Forum in 2016, the UAE topped the rank in the index of women's enrollment in higher education.[4] Similarly, the 2017 annual report by the Center for Arab

---

1   "The UAE: the first Arab country and second globally in terms of security and stability" [in Arabic], Al Ain News, https://al-ain.com/article/the-uae-is-the-most-stable-arab-country

2   "Emirati women," Official Portal of the UAE Government, http://sharik.ae/en/information-and-services/social-affairs/women

3   "The Federal National Council," Official Portal of the UAE Government, https://bit.ly/2PuttjX

4   "The UAE ranks first globally in women's higher education enrollment" [in Arabic], *Al Bayan* (Dubai), December 28, 2016.

Women's Participation Studies, of the Arab Women Studies Center, ranked the UAE, for the third year consecutively, in lead position in terms of women's empowerment.[1]

- Justice and rule of law: The UAE topped the rank in the MENA region, regarding the index of the rule of law around the world, in the 2017-2018 report issued by the Washington-based International Justice Project; thus, ranking ahead of Greece, Hungary, Malaysia, Croatia, and Brazil, among others.[2]

- Government efficiency: The UAE ranked first regionally and tenth globally in the World Competitiveness Yearbook 2017, issued by the Institute for Management Development's World Competitiveness Center in Switzerland. The results showed that the UAE in 2017 advanced five places in the ranking compared to 2016.[3]

- Accountability and transparency: The UAE ranked first in the Arab world, and 21st globally, among 180 countries worldwide, in anti-corruption efforts, according

---

1 See: "Arab Women Foundation Report: UAE 1st in Arab world and in advanced standing in women's rights" [in Arabic], *Al Bayan* (Dubai), January 19, 2018.

2 World Justice Project, *Rule of Law Index, 2017–2018*, https://bit.ly/2DQFeQd

3 IMD World Digital Competitiveness Ranking 2017, https://bit.ly/2rsZ5gM

to the 2017 Corruption Perception Index, by Transparency International.[1]

To crown all the above mentioned achievements, the UAE ranked first in the Arab world, and 21st globally in the 2017 World Happiness Index, as indicated in the World Happiness report published by Earth Institute, Columbia University, and conducted under the auspices of the United Nations.[2]

The limited space of this chapter is not enough to list all the indexes that reflect the current status of political development, in its broader sense, in the UAE, as indicated in reports issued by highly-credible international bodies. My remark in this regard is that the UAE has adopted its own approach to achieve political development, and the key indicator of its success in achieving this development is that the legitimacy of governance has reached its highest levels. This has been clearly manifested in the Emirati people's loyalty to their leaders, rallying around them and supporting their actions and policies, at both internal and external levels. The Emiratis' attitude toward the UAE's participation in the operation to restore legitimacy in Yemen, and the fallen martyrs during this operation, are highly revealing in this regard.

---

1   Transparency International website: https://bit.ly/2BJaDBF

2   See the report, John Helliwell, Richard Layard, and Jeffrey Sachs, eds. *World Happiness Report 2017*. New York: Sustainable Development Solutions Network, 2017. http://worldhappiness.report/ed/2017/

The political literature refers to crises facing the political development process, including identity crisis, legitimacy crisis, participation crisis, penetration crisis, distribution crisis, and integration crisis;[1] however, the facts presented in this chapter clearly emphasize that the UAE is not subject to any of these crises. This indicates that the country has managed to successfully adopt a political development model suitable to its circumstances, and that corresponds to its overall development goals, which is a major source of the UAE's stability and security.

---

1   Aisha Abash, *The Problem of Political Development and Democracy in the Arab Maghreb Countries: Tunisia as a Model* [in Arabic] (Berlin: Democratic Arabic Center for Strategic, Political, and Economic Studies, 2017), pp. 27-29.

7

UAE Society and Change:
Challenges and Opportunities

"Our forefathers contributed to the building of this country, and our duty is to build for future generations, and to follow in the steps of our ancestors. We must take advantage of all experiences without shame and take from them as much as we need, insofar as it is consistent with our traditions and Arab ideals."

Zayed bin Sultan Al Nahyan

M y study, *United Arab Emirates Society: A Future Perspective*,[1] addressed the future of UAE society within its regional and international environment in 2003, as well as the vast, rapid changes and transformations affecting it. At the time, my particular focus was on the issue of globalization and how it affected the identity, culture, customs, and traditions of UAE society. It was the most prominent issue in academia at the time,[2] in addition to technological developments, especially in the field of telecommunications, and their implications on UAE society.

Back then, the world was witnessing the beginning of the so-called communications revolution.[3] However, human history has never witnessed, in terms of magnitude, speed, and timescale,[4] the changes and transformations that have taken place in the world since 2003 in science and

---

1 Jamal Sanad Al-Suwaidi, *United Arab Emirates Society: A Future Perspective* [in Arabic], Emirates Lectures Series, no. 71 (Abu Dhabi: Emirates Center for Strategic Studies and Research, 2003).

2 Galal Amin, *Globalization* [in Arabic] (Cairo: Dar Al-Shorouq, 2008), p. 11.

3 For more details on the communications revolution, its meanings and dimensions, see: Osama Sameer Hussein, *Computer and Communications Revolution* [in Arabic] (Amman: Dar Al Janadriyyah for Publishing and Distribution, 2011).

4 Jamal Dawood Salman, *Knowledge Economy* [in Arabic] (Amman: Dar Al-Yazouri for Publishing and Distribution, 2012), p. 68. See also: Sa'ad Taha Allam, *Development and Society* [in Arabic] (Cairo: Madbouli Library, 2006), p. 88. Also, Ahmad Al-Mansouri, "The Future of Technology: Fact and Fiction" [in Arabic], *Al-Ittihad* (Abu Dhabi), March 18, 2014.

technology. The rate of technological innovation has changed.[1] What is now achieved in a few years would have taken decades, perhaps even centuries, in the past. All of this is due to the open horizons of science that have no boundaries or limits. The ability to innovate, create, and amaze has become greater than can be imagined, or expected, as knowledge has become one of the most important manifestations of wealth and its components.[2]

Undoubtedly, these changes and transformations have a direct impact on UAE society, perhaps more so than any other Arab country. The main reason for this is that the UAE is one of the Arab countries that is most open to and engaged with the world and its technological developments.[3] It is keen to take part in these interactions and developments and contribute to the process of change in the world in all areas, especially at the scientific and

---

1 Jamal Sanad Al-Suwaidi, *Events That Changed History* [in Arabic] (Abu Dhabi, 2018), p. 241.

2 Ibid. pp. 241-242. See also, Mahmoud Mohammad Hussein, *Wealth of Knowledge and Making Wealth: How the Wealth of Nations Is Made?* [in Arabic] (Cairo: The General Authority of the National Library and Archives in cooperation with the Supreme Council of Culture, 2003).

3 I referred to this in my speech at the opening of the 19th Annual Conference of the ECSSR in 2014 under the title "Technology: Impacts, Challenges and the Future." I said, "The UAE is interested, perhaps more than developed countries, in following the technological developments in the world. It is one of the countries in the region and the world that is the most interested in engaging in the digital age, the transition to a knowledge-based economy, innovation, and information technology." See, "The UAE's interest in technological development surpasses developed countries" [in Arabic], *Al Ittihad* (Abu Dhabi), 19 March 2014.

technological level. We note here the interest that the late Sheikh Zayed bin Sultan Al Nahyan (may God rest his soul in peace) had in this issue since the early 1970s. He reiterated to an American journalist, Ms. Fonda, on November 19, 1972, the importance of utilizing useful sciences from modern civilization. He said, "I am not saying that we have to move away from modern civilization. We want things from it. I want to benefit from its advantages, and steer away from the disadvantages...We want science, we want culture, we want the expertise we need everywhere to help us achieve the development of our country. Our goal is to build a generation that can shoulder its responsibilities in building its own country. We want a generation that retains its authentic customs and traditions."[1]

In this context, the National Advanced Sciences Agenda 2031[2] was launched in April 2018. It aims to employ advanced science in developing and creating solutions to future challenges, and supporting the government's efforts in realizing the goals of the national agenda of Vision 2021 and UAE Centennial 2071, by supporting science and sectors related to science and technology

---

1 "Interview of Sheikh Zayed bin Sultan Al Nahyan with the American journalist, Ms. Fonda" [in Arabic] *Al-Ittihad* (Abu Dhabi), November 19, 1972.

2 "National Advanced Sciences Agenda 2031," Official Portal of the UAE Government, https://bit.ly/2wCP5mr

outcomes, through three sequential strategies, starting with 2018-2021.

The UAE National Advanced Sciences Agenda 2031 is based on utilizing science to find solutions to challenges and to explore economically viable opportunities by working on eight scientific priorities up to 2031 and 30 scientific goals up to 2021.[1] Additionally, the UAE is one of the countries interested in foreseeing the future, preparing for its changes and developments, and developing plans and strategies to deal with it. In this context, the UAE has set a number of strategies and initiatives, including UAE Vision 2021,[2] UAE Centennial 2071,[3] UAE Future Strategy,[4] Global Future Councils,[5] UAE Future Foresight Platform,[6] and Mohamed bin Zayed Council for Future Generations.[7] Further, in 2016, the

---

1   "National Advanced Sciences Agenda 2031," The Official Portal of the UAE Government, https://bit.ly/2wCP5mr

2   "UAE Vision 2021," https://www.vision2021.ae

3   "UAE Centennial 2071," https://area2071.ae/

4   "UAE Future Strategy," Ministry of Cabinet Affairs and the Future, https://bit.ly/2oeAjyd

5   Global Future Councils, https://bit.ly/2ylNHnC

6   UAE Future Foresight Platform, https://uaefutureforesight.ae

7   Huda Al-Kubaisi, "Mohamed bin Zayed Council for Future Generations: An Arena for Creativity Led by Youth" [in Arabic], Emirates News Agency, March 8, 2017, http://wam.ae/ar/details/1395302601806

Ministry of Cabinet Affairs was renamed the Ministry of Cabinet Affairs and the Future.[1]

Looking at the implications of the global change on UAE society, it can be said that it is both challenging and full of opportunity. No one can argue that there are many challenges and risks to UAE society stemming from technological, social, and cultural changes in the world. The first is the danger it poses to national identity.[2] The revolution in communication and information has not only brought to the UAE advanced technological devices that facilitated the communication between citizens and the world, and opened the doors of knowledge without limits, but it also came with ideas, values, cultures, customs and behavior; some of which are positive and some negative. All of this has influenced our national identity, the system of values, and social behavior, especially among the youth, who are more involved in utilizing the technologies of the information revolution, and more attracted to the cultures, arts, and foreign values accompanying this revolution.

---

1 "Future Foresight," Ministry of Cabinet Affairs and the Future, https://bit.ly/2Lu9gIs

2 For details on the threats of change to identity, refer to Chapter 5 of this book (Jamal Sanad Al-Suwaidi, *United Arab Emirates Society in the Twenty-first Century: Issues and Challenges in a Changing World*, Abu Dhabi, 2018), titled "National Identity: Significance and Sources of Threats."

Perhaps the most serious impact, in my view, of the changes the world is inflicting on our identity is the threat to the Arabic language. The use of this language is, worryingly, being replaced by foreign languages, especially English, which children and the youth accept as the language of science in the world and one of the most important requirements of the labor market.[1]

Learning foreign languages, English or other, is essential and must be encouraged, but it should not be at the expense of Arabic. There are models of several countries in the world that have reached the ranks of developed countries without giving up their language, culture or identity—Japan, South Korea, and Singapore are such examples.[2]

The UAE has taken many measures to preserve the Arabic language, most notably the decision of the Cabinet

---

1   "Arabic is forgotten in Universities… and 90% of the students are unsatisfied with school classes" [in Arabic], *Emarat Alyoum* (Dubai), December 26, 2016. In a poll by the UAE Ministry of Education, 19 percent of the respondents felt that children's weakness in the Arabic language is due to the dominance of colloquial Arabic, while 19 percent felt the reason to be the lack of attractive Arabic books. 12 percent said that parents are the reason, while 50 percent attributed the weakness in Arabic to the spread of the English language. See, "Ministry of Education Poll: English is the main reason for weakness in Arabic" [in Arabic], *Al Bayan* (Dubai) April 24, 2017. For more details on the effect of Globalization on Arabic see, Mohammad Yousef Al-Hazaymeh, *Cultural Globalization and Arabic: Challenges and Impacts* [in Arabic] (Amman: Academic Publishing and Distribution, 2012).

2   Jamal Sanad Al-Suwaidi, *Events That Changed History* [in Arabic] (Abu Dhabi, 2018), p. 247.

on March 9, 2008 to adopt Arabic as an official language in government institutions and bodies.[1] The Constitution also states that, "The Union shall be part of the Great Arab Nation, to which it is bound by the ties of religion, language, history and common destiny. The people of the Union shall be a single people, and shall be part of the Arab Nation,"[2] and that, "Islam shall be the official religion of the Union. The Islamic Sharia shall be a principal source of legislation in the Union. The official language of the Union shall be Arabic."[3]

Nevertheless, this has not prevented the decline of the Arabic language in the face of other languages, especially English, which is common in many Arab countries, not only in the UAE.[4]

In addition to language, one of the serious aspects of the impact of change in the world on our identity is the system of values. For example, the communications revolution has brought with it consumer and individual

---

1 "UAE marks Arabic language Day" [in Arabic], *Al-Ittihad* (Abu Dhabi), February 27, 2011. For more details on UAE initiatives to preserve the Arabic language see, "UAE leads initiatives to preserve Arabic" [in Arabic], *Al Bayan* (Dubai) December 17, 2017.

2 Article 6 of the Constitution of the United Arab Emirates.

3 Article 7 of the Constitution of the United Arab Emirates.

4 In this regard see, Arafah Mohammad Mohammad Khair, "Weakness in Arabic in the Colleges of Education: Reasons, Effects, and Proposed Remedies" [in Arabic] (paper presented at the Third Arabic Language Conference, Dubai, May 8-10, 2014), https://bit.ly/2I6YXJr

values[1] that have superseded the concepts of integration, solidarity, and social and family solidarity, which have been characteristics of UAE society for years.

The second challenge posed by modern day changes is the economic threat, or challenge. In light of the major technological developments in the field of energy, which is expected to increase in the coming years, the importance of fossil fuel-based energy, represented by oil, is declining. There is talk about the end of the oil era,[2] which is the mainstay of the economy in the UAE. Hence, the decline in global demand for oil will have different impacts on UAE society, especially with regard to the standard of living, welfare, and employment (unemployment rates), and other aspects that will have complex social implications that must be carefully studied and tackled with interest.

Third, there is the security challenge. In the face of sweeping technological development, there has been an increase in the risk of cybercrime and cyber-based and technology-based attacks,[3] which could be even more powerful

---

1   Azzam Mohammad Al-Juwaili, *Social Media* [in Arabic] (Amman: Dar Ghaida' Publishing and Distribution, 2014), p. 79.

2   David Goodstein, *Out of Gas: The End of the Age of Oil* (New York: W. W. Norton & Company, 2005), pp. 117-120.

3   For more details on the danger of these crimes see, Richard Clarke and Robert Knake, *Cyber War: The Next Threat to National Security and What to Do about It* (New York: Ecco, 2011). Also, John Bassett, "Cyber Warfare: Offensive and Defensive," in *The Future of Warfare in the 21st Century* (Abu Dhabi: Emirates Center for Strategic Studies and Research, 2014), pp. 53-67.

and dangerous than military attacks. In its 2017 report, the European Police Agency (Europol) said that technology is used in almost all organized crime, and that criminals utilize artificial intelligence to carry out their crimes.[1] A report prepared by McAfee for information security programs, in cooperation with the Center for Strategic and International Studies in Washington DC in February 2018, said that because of cybercrime, the world economy suffered an annual loss of US$600 billion, accounting for about 1 percent of global gross domestic product (GDP).[2]

Moreover, the role of social media and the communications revolution in influencing the minds of young people has increased. This threatens to turn them into a source of instability, especially as UAE society is a young society[3] and young people are the most connected to the world and affected by what is going on, whether negative or positive.

Fourth, changes taking place in the world do not exclude any sector. Rather, they are comprehensive and

---

1 For more details, see: "Serious and Organized Crime... Threat Assessment, Crime in The Age of Technology," https://bit.ly/2na2zQR.

2 Lewis James, "Economic Impact of Cybercrime—No Slowing Down," https://bit.ly/ 2EMuUtb

3 Youth represent around 50 percent of the UAE population. See, "Mohammed bin Rashed: UAE is a young country that builds its future depending on the youth" [in Arabic], *Al-Ittihad* (Abu Dhabi), April 11, 2016. See also, "Youth," Official Portal of the UAE Government, https://bit.ly/2LNX05N

radical, as previously mentioned. This means that we, in the UAE, are required to develop new visions for education, health, technology, security, economy, transport, and in every other field, so that we can cope with these changes.

In this regard, the challenges facing us are increasing. In recent years, our cadres have received education, training, and qualifications, all of which need to be reconsidered because the future needs a different quality of education, training, qualification and human resources. The professions of the future will be different—new jobs will emerge, existing jobs will disappear, areas of work that do not exist now will come about, and companies and institutions will disappear if they are unable to develop themselves to cope with change in the world.

In light of the gravity of the previous challenges associated with the process of change in the world, it is fortunate that the UAE leadership sees change not only as a challenge but also as an opportunity that must be invested in and leveraged to maximize gains and reduce risks. Our leadership believes that the best way for any country to meet the challenges of change and rationalize its course is to be at the heart of this change, not far away from it or on its margins.

In this context, many plans and strategies have been announced, all of which aim to ensure that the UAE keeps up with the international scientific and technological revolution, as well as actively contribute to it. This is reflected in the UAE Strategy for the Fourth Industrial Revolution,[1] launched in September 2017, which focuses on several main pillars:

First, the human of the future; improving educational results by focusing on advanced sciences and technologies (e.g., bioengineering, nanotechnology, and artificial intelligence).

Second, adopting plans and strategies in the fields of genomic medicine and genomic medical tourism through improving health care and developing personalized medical solutions and genomic medicine according to the patients' needs.

Third, focusing on "Robo Care," by harnessing clinical robots and nanotechnology to augment the UAE's health-care capabilities and provide remote robotic medical services and intelligent healthcare interventions through wearable and implantable technologies.

Fourth, the security of the future. Developing a sustainable food and water ecosystem by leveraging bio-engineering, advanced sciences, and technologies, as well as renewable energy.

Fifth, enhancing economic security by adopting a digital economy, and digital technological interactions.

---

1 "The UAE Strategy for the Fourth Industrial Revolution," Official Portal of the UAE Government, https://bit.ly/2MwhTYp

Sixth, encouraging entrepreneurship of the future through investing in space research, and consolidating the position of the UAE as a global hub for ambitious space participants in the areas of research, projects, and investment.

Seventh, supporting national research and application efforts in universities and specialized centers in the field of neuroscience and human enhancement, in collaboration with global leaders in the field.[1]

In addition to the above, the Fourth Industrial Revolution Council,[2] and the Emirates Scientists Council[3] were established. The Fourth Industrial Revolution Protocol was launched[4] in 2017, in collaboration with the World Economic Forum. The protocol consists of three main pillars—providing a comprehensive and safe environment for data, drafting the policies and legislations of the Fourth Industrial Revolution (4IR), and developing a system of values and ethics of the 4IR.

---

1 "The UAE Strategy for the Fourth Industrial Revolution," The Official Portal of the UAE Government, https://bit.ly/2MwhTYp.

2 "UAE: Pioneers Initiatives Based on Future Technology" [in Arabic], *Akhbar Al Saah*, (Abu Dhabi: Emirates Center for Strategic Studies and Research, September 24, 2017). https://bit.ly/2QXNQaH

3 Emirates Scientists Council, http://www.sc.gov.ae/home-en

4 "UAE launches Fourth Industrial Revolution Protocol," *Gulf News* (Dubai), November 12, 2017, https://bit.ly/2MAt7eC

Furthermore, there is the Mars 2117 UAE space project,[1] the first of its kind in the Arab world, which aims to establish the first inhabitable human settlement on Mars.[2] There is also the National Strategy for Innovation,[3] which involves several plans and programs of action aimed at promoting innovation and creativity in different sectors of the UAE through: first, creating an environment conducive to innovation; second, developing government innovation; third, driving the private sector toward greater innovation; and fourth, developing individuals who possess advanced entrepreneurial skills.

This is in addition to the important steps that have been taken in the field of education development as the real and fundamental input to progress and active involvement in the 4IR in all its aspects, including the Strategy of the Ministry of Education 2010-2020,[4] Higher Education Strategy 2030,[5] the strategies for developing national human resources, and the preparation of future generations to deal with the changes in the world of

---

1   "The UAE 2030-2117," Official Portal of the UAE Government, https://government.ae/en/more/uae-future/2030-2117

2   Ibid.

3   "National Strategy for Innovation," Ministry of Cabinet Affairs and the Future, 2015, https://bit.ly/2NlTaCt

4   "New education strategy includes 50 initiatives," *Gulf News* (Dubai), February 24, 2010, https://bit.ly/2PN0OHt

5   "National Strategy for Higher Education 2030," Ministry of Education website, https://bit.ly/2LBzYz4

tomorrow on the level of education, jobs, and services. Moreover, there are many other ideas and plans that reflect that our leadership is well aware of the nature of changes taking place in the world, and the position we aspire to reach within it.

Moreover, while recognizing the negative effects that changes in the world have had on UAE society, I believe these changes, especially the social and cultural ones, will probably not pose a serious threat to social stability in the UAE for many reasons. First, UAE society has been open to the world for a long time,[1] and this makes it able to deal with the changes coming from abroad in a positive and balanced way. Conversely, closed societies will face a flood of transitions, ideas, and values that come from outside the borders without the experience to deal with them, which exposes them to deep problems and threats, or what can be called the "shock of modernity,"[2] especially since the magnitude of global change leaves no opportunity for reflection, nor does it allow a margin of choice or hesitation.

---

1   Yousef Al-Salem, *Sheikh Mohammed bin Rashed Al Maktoum on the National, Arab, and International Levels* [in Arabic] (Dubai: Dar Al Hudhud for Publishing and Distribution, 2016), p. 205.

2   For a definition of the 'shock of modernity,' see, Mohammad Sbeela, "Modernity and Modernization in Contemporary Western Thought: Part 1" [in Arabic], Arab Scientific Center for Research and Humanities Studies website, https://bit.ly/2Ir9iDy

Second, UAE society has eliminated many of the problems faced by Arab and Muslim societies in dealing with global transformations, especially problems related to the role of women and their position in society, the role of religion and its outlook, and the perception of the other. The role of women, their contribution, and their participation in society and public affairs are no longer controversial or a topic for discussion. Hence, the UAE has attained top international rankings in the field of women's empowerment according to specialized international indicators, including the Women Peace and Security Index 2017–2018, issued by the Oslo Peace Research Institute and Georgetown Institute for Women, Peace and Security. These put the UAE in first place in the Arab and Islamic world and 42nd globally in terms of the wellbeing and empowerment of women.[1]

There is a clear and balanced vision toward religion in UAE society, which does not confuse it with terrorist organizations. According to a poll conducted by the Zogby Institute in Washington, 89 percent of UAE youth believe religion is important in society. At the same time, 80 percent of them see extremist and terrorist organizations as

---

1 Georgetown Institute for Women, Peace and Security and Peace Research Institute Oslo. *Women, Peace and Security Index 2017/18: Tracking Sustainable Peace through Inclusion, Justice, and Security for Women.* Washington, DC: GIWPS and PRIO, 2017, p. 17, https://bit.ly/2j2egIY

a "complete perversion of Islam."[1] Another poll, conducted by the ECSSR between December 10 and 16, 2017, reiterated a similar viewpoint. The poll, on the position of UAE nationals toward the Muslim Brotherhood, found that 97.55 percent of the respondents generally have an extremely negative or negative view of the Muslim Brotherhood.[2]

Undoubtedly, the issues of women, religion, and sect are still ones that hinder many societies from positive involvement in the world's changes and transformations, and plunge them into futile debates that exhaust their efforts, divide them, and make them spin in vicious circles while the world develops and moves forward at an unprecedented speed.

Third, for many years, UAE society has recognized technology in its various dimensions, both the positive and negative, and dealt with them rationally. For example, Dubai Internet City was established in 1999, the UAE launched the e-Dirham in 2001, and Dubai Silicon Oasis Authority in 2005. In 2011, Abu Dhabi was the first capital in the world to be covered by a fiber optic network.

---

1   James Zogby, "Muslim Millennials' Views on Religion," Huff Post, January 9, 2016. https://bit.ly/2oish7F.

2   "98% of Emiratis reject Muslim Brotherhood," *Khaleej Times* (Dubai), January 14, 2018.

In addition, there are other initiatives such as Smart Government and e-government.[1]

Fourth, for many years the UAE leadership has been preparing to deal with change, putting scientific and technological changes at the heart of these plans. The late Sheikh Zayed bin Sultan Al Nahyan (may God rest his soul in peace) realized the importance of technology and the significance of localizing it as the foundation for advancement and involvement in the modern-age process. Therefore, he said, "Science is the only way toward advancement, facing the current challenges, and serving development in developing countries. The UAE is keen on taking part in supporting the development strategy and transferring technology to the Third World countries."[2]

In this context, the UAE leadership has for a long time been intent on building a strong technological base that depends on both importing technology as well as localizing and producing it.[3]

Fifth, the UAE has been keen on keeping all development, modernization, and openness to the world

---

1 Ahmed Majid, *Innovation Enhancement Mechanisms in the UAE* [in Arabic], UAE Ministry of Economy, 2017, pp. 16-19, https://goo.gl/4b1DzX

2 "Under the patronage of Hazza bin Zayed...'Abu Dhabi Technical' Organizes Technical Education and Innovation Week" [in Arabic], Emirates News Agency, January 23, 2018, https://bit.ly/2Lk772E

3 For more details on the UAE's attention to technology, see: "Key sectors in science and technology," Official Portal of the UAE Government, https://bit.ly/2NEcVW7

within the frame of heritage, traditions, and cultural specificities. This has created an open society that is actively involved in globalization and the communications and technological revolution; yet, it stays in touch with its heritage and identity.[1]

Undoubtedly, for these five reasons, UAE society is more confident in the way it views change. On the one hand, it has surpassed several Arab and Islamic societies in dealing with change; on the other, it is seriously preparing for active involvement, as previously pointed out.

---

1 "Efforts of the UAE Government in preserving the heritage," Official Portal of the UAE Government, https://bit.ly/2MZGSCM.

Conclusion

"It is essential to give more attention to all issues concerning the security, stability, and welfare of society, and to exert more efforts to strengthen the Union, at home and abroad, to achieve what every citizen aspires to, and to work for the benefit of the nation and its stability and security."

Zayed bin Sultan Al Nahyan

In this book, I have discussed issues relating to UAE society from different perspectives, based on four pillars or elements.

The **first element** is to look at UAE society within the broader context of the regional and international environment, as well as the developments and changes affecting societies in all countries of the world, especially those strongly involved in the process of modernization and globalization, such as UAE society.

This is extremely important in light of the communications and information revolution, the great openness between peoples and cultures, and the changes in the concept of borders in their traditional sense. Our society does not live on an isolated island. What happens in our environment, whether regional or international, affects us one way or the other. Therefore, studying and understanding this external environment is vital to grasping the opportunities it offers our society to carry on the process of development, advancement, and progress, and to identify the challenges it poses to us and how to confront them.

The leadership of the UAE has demonstrated a great ability to understand the external variables surrounding our society, how to integrate securely with the international community, and transform the UAE into a global model that many countries and societies are trying to emulate.

The **second element** is to trace the historical roots that have shaped the identity of UAE society and have deeply influenced it. Their impact remains long lasting and renewed. Hence, my focus is on the impact of the UAE experience on the structure of the society, especially as the experience of development and modernization in the UAE has, from the beginning, been based on blending originality and modernity, or being actively open to the world while preserving heritage, values, customs, and traditions.

The **third element** is to link the different aspects that I have addressed in this book to the future. In other words, how the fast-paced changes in the world around us will affect UAE society, and how these changes can be handled, both during the current phase and in the future. The importance of this is that the UAE is a country that shows great interest in looking ahead and is keen to prepare society to deal with changes and transformations on all levels.

The **fourth element** is that I did not look at UAE society from a narrow perspective, limited to the social aspect; rather, I expanded the angle, or angles, of the approach to include political, economic, security, cultural and other dimensions on the basis that society is affected by, and in turn influences, all of them.

In this context, I dedicated a section to discussing the changes taking place in the UAE toward the adoption of a knowledge-based economic model, which will have an important impact on UAE society in the 21st century. Hence, there is a need to build human resources with skills and knowledge-based expertise, and ensure they are equipped with the values of innovation and creativity to maintain our progress and our pioneering experience. I also devoted a special section to education and its importance in capacity-building and preparing human resources qualified to lead sustainable development in the future, including the safe transition into the post-oil era.

I shed light on the political development experience in the UAE—an experience that safeguarded the political stability we enjoy in this country. The political development experience was based on promoting the values of citizenship, transparency, accountability, and the empowerment of women; yet, first and foremost, it was centered on realizing the happiness and wellbeing of UAE citizens.

In this book, I have provided a comprehensive overview of what I believe to be the priorities and challenges of UAE society, and I have attempted to set some important milestones on the way to the future when addressing such priorities and challenges; nonetheless, I call for more attention to studies related to UAE society. However, the focus on political, security, and strategic issues, although necessary, important, and justifiable, should not neglect the social dimensions of these issues, nor deprive them the attention and focus they deserve. There are many reasons that lead me to make such a call:

First, social security is one of the most important and most dangerous aspects of national security in its broadest sense. It is also closely linked to all other aspects of national security—political, cultural, economic, and others. In fact, one cannot discuss social security in any society in isolation from the political, economic, cultural, technological, and security developments and variables in this society.

Second, UAE society has undergone great changes and transformations, on multiple levels, in recent years, which need numerous studies to examine them, analyze them, show their different effects on the security and identity of the society, and learn about the lessons they present for future challenges and priorities.

Several studies have been conducted recently on the influence that economic changes have had (especially the oil factor) on the structure, culture, and identity of UAE society. However, the issue still needs further study and research, because the transformations are large, continuous, and accelerating, and their ramifications and effects are complex.

Third, the future holds a lot for society in the UAE, especially as it is interested in the prospects of this future and is prepared, as previously mentioned, to deal with it through changes and transformations on many levels and in many areas. This entails important social implications that require further research and study from specialists in the fields of sociology, security, politics, and others.

In this context, I believe that the last chapter of this book, titled "UAE society and Change: Challenges and Opportunities," represents an important basis that can be built upon and used as a springboard to undertake many comprehensive studies on UAE society, and issues of change—issues that are varied, yet complex at the same time.

Fourth, the impact of the Fourth Industrial Revolution (4IR), which the world, including the UAE, is living through, is not limited to technological or scientific-technical aspects; it also extends to many other aspects, especially the social one. The UAE is one of the countries keen to engage in the course of the Fourth Industrial Revolution (4IR), which needs in-depth scientific studies on the social repercussions of this revolution on UAE society, especially at the level of values, relations, and priorities.

Fifth, the UAE's early readiness to enter the post-oil era, with its accompanying changes, particularly at the level of the welfare-state model, as well as changes in the nature of the national economy, are all variables that have profound social implications and require intensive follow-up research by specialists in this area.

Sixth, the new generations of wars, as previously mentioned, aim to destroy communities from within by provoking the causes of tension and instability within them. This makes social research related to the security, peace, and development of societies a high priority, especially in a regional and international environment suffering from the spread of religious, ethnic, and sectarian groups, casting their negative influence on societies, their security, and the coexistence of their people.

The UAE has succeeded through the decades in staying out of sectarian, ethnic, factional, and religious conflicts, fortifying its society in the face of attempts to destroy communities from within through Fourth-Generation Warfare (4GW). However, the threats to society are constantly changing and renewed under the major transformations that affect the nature of warfare and its tools, in both regional and international arenas. In turn, this requires comprehensive studies and research on the sources of danger that threaten society in the present and future, and how to deal with them and address their evils.

Seventh, great economic transformations are ac-companied by great social transformations as well; this is the case in the UAE, which has ambitious economic and development plans, directly affecting the nature of society.

Over the past half century, UAE society has succeeded in striking a balance between preserving its identity, values, and heritage, on the one hand, and, on the other hand, creating its own development and modernization model, which has become a global model many countries are trying to emulate. The ability to enter the future confidently and safely, based on the same equation (preservation of identity and continuation of development and modernization), has been possible not only because of a political leadership that has the vision and will to place this society in its earned position among civilized nations, but also because this society, when the late Sheikh Zayed bin Sultan Al Nahyan (may God rest his soul in peace) and his brothers the Rulers of the Emirates established it, was founded on the will to challenge and achieve it. This was done on the basis of a unique national harmony and cohesion between the leadership and the people, which will safeguard the society's security, stability, and renaissance for decades and centuries to come. The solid foundation of UAE society is the guarantee of continuity and progress in the near and distant future.

In conclusion, the achievements by the late Sheikh Zayed bin Sultan Al Nahyan (may God rest his soul in peace) are numerous, the most important of which is that he was able to give the people of the UAE one identity.

Bibliography

Abash, Aisha. *The Problem of Political Development and Democracy in the Arab Maghreb Countries: Tunisia as a Model* [in Arabic]. Berlin: Democratic Arabic Center for Strategic, Political, and Economic Studies, 2017.

Abdullah Al-Raisi, "The Development Dimension of Education in the UAE" [in Arabic]. In *Education and Development: Investing in the Future*. Abu Dhabi: Emirates Center for Strategic Studies and Research, 2017.

Abell, Angela and Nigel Oxbrow. *Competing with Knowledge*. London: Library Association Publishing, 2001.

Abou Zekri, Wajih. *Zayed from Near* [in Arabic]. Cairo: Dar Akhbar El Yom, 1991.

Aboud, Rami. *The Arabic Digital Content on the Internet* [in Arabic]. Cairo: Al Arabi Publishing and Distributing, 2013.

Abrash, Ibrahim. *Political Sociology: An Epistemological Approach and an Applied Study on the Arab World* [in Arabic]. London: E-Kutub Ltd., 2011.

Abul-Ela, Mohamed Hussein. *Religious Violence in Egypt: A Reading in Islamic Thought* [in Arabic]. Cairo: Mahrousa Center for Publishing, Press Services and Information, 2007.

Abu-Nasr, Medhat and Yasmin Medhat Mohammed. *Sustainable Development: Concept, Dimensions, and Indicators* [in Arabic]. Cairo: Arab Group for Training and publishing, 2017.

Ahmed, Ahmed Yousef et al. *Future of Change in the Arab World* [in Arabic]. Beirut: Center for Arab Unity Studies, 2016.

Ahmed, Mustafa. *The Global Conspiracy. Fourth Generation Warfare: The Modern Application of the Protocols of the Elders of Zion* [in Arabic]. Cairo: El-Sherif Mass Publication and Distribution, 2017.

Al Khazaleh, Fatima Ahmed. *Communications and Education Technology* [in Arabic]. Amman: Dar Al-Majd Publishing and Distribution, 2014.

Al Maktoum, Mohammed bin Rashid, *Reflections on Happiness and Positivity* [in Arabic]. Dubai: Explorer Publishing & Distribution LLC, 2017.

_____. *Flashes of Thought: Inspired by a Dialogue at the Government Summit 2013* [in Arabic]. Dubai: Kuttab Publishing House, 2013.

Al Mazrouei, Mariam. *Zayed and Women's Education in Abu Dhabi* [in Arabic]. Dubai: Kuttab Publishing House, 2015.

Al-Aani, Khalil Nouri. *Islamic Identity in the Age of Cultural Globalization* [in Arabic]. Baghdad: Sunni Endowment Diwan, 2009.

Al-Ahmad, Wassim Husam Al-Din. *Women's and Children's Rights in Light of the Gulf Legislation and Regulations* [in Arabic]. Riyadh: Law and Economics Library, 2015.

Al-Arshani, Awad. *The Life of Zayed: The Knight Who Conquered the Desert* [in Arabic]. Cairo: n. p., 1980.

Al-Azi, Sweilem. *Sheikh Zayed and His Role in the Emergence and Development of the UAE* [in Arabic]. Amman: Academic Book Center, 2015.

Al-Dhafiri, Fahad Mishary. *Globalization and National Identity* [in Arabic]. Kuwait: Dar Qurtas Publishing, 2002.

Al-Ethawi, Wissam Hussein Ali. *Modernization and Stability in the Iraqi Political System after 2003* [in Arabic]. Berlin: Democratic Arabic Center for Strategic, Political, and Economic Studies, 2018.

Al-Falahi, Hussein Ali Ibrahim. *New Globalization: Dimensions and Repercussions* [in Arabic]. Amman: Dar Ghaida' Publishing and Distribution, 2014.

Al-Hariri, Jassem. *Israeli Schemes to Dismantle the Arab Region: Iraq 1948-2013, A Case Study* [in Arabic]. Amman: Dar Al-Jenan Books, 2014.

Al-Hazaymeh, Mohammad Yousef. *Cultural Globalization and Arabic: Challenges and Impacts* [in Arabic]. Amman: Academic Publishing and Distribution, 2012.

Al-Jazrawi, Rashid Abbas. *The Phenomenon of Globalization and Its Impact on Unemployment in the Arab World* [in Arabic]. Amman: Academic Book Center, 2015.

Al-Juboori, Musleh Khader. *The Roots of Arab Oppression and the Arab Spring* [in Arabic]. Amman: Academics for Publishing and Distribution, 2013.

Al-Juwaili, Azzam Mohammad. *Social Media* [in Arabic]. Amman: Dar Ghaida' Publishing and Distribution, 2014.

Al-Khazraji, Thamer Kamel Mohammed. *Modern Political Systems and Public Policies: A Contemporary Study of the Power Management Strategy* [in Arabic]. Amman: Majdalawi for Publishing and Distribution, 2004.

Allam, Sa'ad Taha. *Development and Society* [in Arabic]. Cairo: Madbouli Library, 2006.

Al-Madfa'i, Yousef Mohammad. *Zayed and the UAE: Building the Union State* [in Arabic]. Abu Dhabi: Abu Dhabi Authority for Culture and Heritage, 2008.

Al-Maqdisi, Abdullah bin Ahmed Ibn Qudamah. *Rawdat al Nather fi Jannet al Manather* [in Arabic]. Riyadh: Al Roshd Library, N.D.

Al-Mukhtar, Salah. *America's Syndrome: Is it an Arab Spring or the Second Sykes-Picot?* [in Arabic]. London: E-Book Ltd., 2016.

Al-Rbei'awi, Sa'doun Hmoud and Hussein Waleed Abbas. *Intellectual Capital* [in Arabic]. Amman: Dar Ghaida' Publishing and Distribution, 2015.

Al-Salem, Yousef. *Sheikh Mohammed bin Rashed Al Maktoum on the National, Arab, and International Levels* [in Arabic]. Dubai: Dar Al Hudhud for Publishing and Distribution, 2016.

Al-Salmi, Ali. *Management in the Age of Knowledge and Globalization* [in Arabic]. Cairo: Sama Publishing Production, and Distribution, 2014.

Al-Shamsi, Abdullatif. "Vision 2.0: Together Toward the UAE Centennial" [in Arabic]. In *Education and Development: Investing in the Future*. Abu Dhabi: Emirates Center for Strategic Studies and Research, 2017.

Al-Suwaidi, Jamal Sanad. *Eternal Imprints: Figures That Made History and Others That Changed the Future of Their Countries*. Abu Dhabi, 2016.

—————. *Events That Changed History* [in Arabic]. Abu Dhabi, 2018.

—————. *Prospects for the American Age: Sovereignty and Influence in the New World Order*. Abu Dhabi, 2014.

—————. *Sheikh Zayed's Approach in Building the Union State* [in Arabic]. Emirates Lectures Series, no. 211. Abu Dhabi: Emirates Center for Strategic Studies and Research, 2018.

—————. *The Mirage*. Abu Dhabi, 2015.

_____. *United Arab Emirates Society: A Future* Perspective [in Arabic]. Emirates Lectures Series, no. 71. Abu Dhabi: Emirates Center for Strategic Studies and Research, 2003.

Al-Taweel, Rawa Zaki. *Sustainable Development in Light of Democracy and Human Rights* [in Arabic]. Amman: Zahran Publishers, 2009.

Amara, Hani Abdel Kader. *Energy and the Age of Power* [in Arabic]. Amman: Dar Ghaida' Publishing and Distribution, 2011.

Amin, Galal. "Globalization and the State." In *Arabs and Globalization: Research and Discussions of the Symposium Organized by the Arab Union Studies Center* [in Arabic]. Beirut: Arab Union Studies Center, 2000.

_____. *Globalization* [in Arabic]. Cairo, Dar Al-Shorouq, 2001.

Amin, Reda. *New Media* [in Arabic]. Cairo: Dar Al-Fajr Publishing and Distribution, 2015.

Bani Ayesh, Mohamed Said. *Modernity from an Islamic Perspective* [in Arabic]. Irbid: Dar Al-Kitab Al-Thaqafi, 2016.

Bashir, Aisha Ahmed, et al. *The Family in the UAE* [in Arabic]. Sharjah: Sociologist Association, 1994.

Bassett, John, "Cyber Warfare: Offensive and Defensive." In *The Future of Warfare in the 21ˢᵗ Century*. Abu Dhabi: Emirates Center for Strategic Studies and Research, 2014.

Bijian, Zheng. *China's Road to Peaceful Rise: Observations on Its Cause, Basis, Connotation and Prospect*. New York: Routledge, 2011.

Burton-Jones, Alan. *Knowledge Capitalism: Business, Work and Learning in the New Economy*. Oxford: Oxford University Press, 1999.

Buteebah, Faisal Ahmed. *Return on Investment in Education* [in Arabic]. Amman: Dar Al-Yazouri for Publishing and Distribution, 2013.

Campbell, Colin et al. *The End of the Age of Oil: Necessary Measures for the Future* [in Arabic]. Kuwait: National Council for Culture, Arts, and Letters, September 2004.

Dada, Robin. "The UAE: A Regional Center for Education" [in Arabic]. In *Education and Development: Investing in the Future*. Abu Dhabi: Emirates Center for Strategic Studies and Research, 2017.

Clarke, Richard and Robert Knake. *Cyber War: The Next Threat to National Security and What to Do about It*. New York: Ecco, 2011.

Dakhlallah, Ayoub. *Education and the Problems of Society in an Era of Globalization* [in Arabic]. Beirut: Dar al-Kotob Al-Ilmiyah, 2015.

El Hanashi, Mohamed El Hadi. *Zayed: The Pioneer of Good* [in Arabic]. Abu Dhabi: Zayed Centre for Coordination & Follow-up, July 2001.

El-Erian, Mohammed. *The Available Game...Disorder of Central Banks and Averting the Next Collapse* [translated into Arabic by Mustafa Mahmoud]. Cairo: Dar Al Kotob Khan, 2018.

Emad, Abdel Ghani. *Sociology of Culture: Concepts and Problematics, From Modernity to Globalization* [in Arabic]. Beirut: Centre for Arab Unity Studies, 2006.

Farouk, Nabeel. *You Are the Army of Your Enemy: Fourth Generation Warfare* [in Arabic]. Cairo: Dar Al Nahda Egypt, 2016.

Fukuyama, Francis. *The End of History and the Last Man*. USA: Free Press, 1992.

Goodstein, David. *Out of Gas: The End of the Age of Oil*. New York: W. W. Norton & Company, 2005.

Harold, Barbara. "The Role of the Private Sector in Supporting Research." In *Education and Development: Toward a Modern Education System in the UAE*. Abu Dhabi: Emirates Center for Strategic Studies and Research, 2018.

Hashem, Tamer Ibrahim Kamel. *The Conflict between the United States of America, and the People's Republic of China and the Russian Federation as Rising Powers: A Case Study of Central Asia and the Caspian Sea* [in Arabic]. Cairo: Al Maktab Al Arabi Lil Maaref, 2014.

Hirst, Paul, Grahame Thompson, and Simon Bromley. *Globalization in Question: The International Economy and the Possibilities of Governance*. Cambridge: Polity Press, 1996.

Huntington, Samuel P. *Political Order in Changing Societies*. Translated into Arabic by Sumaya Flo Abboud. Beirut: Dar Al Saqi, 1993.

_____. *Who Are We? The Challenges to America's National Identity*. London: The Free Press, 2004.

Hussein, Mahmoud Mohammad. *Wealth of Knowledge and Making Wealth: How the Wealth of Nations Is Made?* [in Arabic]. Cairo: The General Authority of the National Library and Archives in cooperation with the Supreme Council of Culture, 2003.

Hussein, Osama Sameer. *Computer and Communications Revolution* [in Arabic]. Amman: Dar Al Janadriyyah for Publishing and Distribution, 2011.

Ibish, Hussein. *The UAE's Evolving National Security Strategy.* Washington: Arab Gulf States Institute in Washington, 2017.

Ibrahim, Saad Eddin. *On the Issue of Unity and the Decline of Pan-Arabism* [in Arabic]. Cairo: Dar Ibn Roshd, 2018.

Ismail, Mohamed Sadiq. *The UAE Experience: Reading in the Federal Experiment* [in Arabic]. Cairo: Al Arabi Publishing & Distribution 2017.

Jabali, Hamza. *Development of Human Resources Management* [in Arabic]. Amman: Dar Alam Thaqafa for Publishing & Distribution, 2016.

Jameel, Abdulkareem Ahmad. *Modern Human Development* [in Arabic]. Amman: Dar Al Janadriyyah for Publishing and Distribution, 2017.

Kafi, Mustafa Yousef. *E-Learning and Knowledge Economy* [in Arabic]. Damascus: Raslan Publishing House, 2009.

Kenana, Ali Nasser. *Culture and Its Manifestations: Surface and Depth* [in Arabic]. Beirut: Al Rihab Publisher Est., 2016.

Khalil, Hasan. *Democracy, Globalization, and Wars* [in Arabic]. Beirut: Dar Al Farabi, 2010.

Lane, Jason E. "The Impact of Branches of Foreign Universities in the UAE." In *The Future of Education in the UAE: Innovation and Knowledge Production.* Abu Dhabi: Emirates Center for Strategic Studies and Research, 2014.

Mahboob, Abdul Hafeez Rahim. *Solid Tackle: Saudi Arabia in the Face of Iranian Impulses* [in Arabic]. London: E-Kutub Ltd., 2017.

Maitra, Jayanti. *Zayed: From Challenges to Union* [in Arabic]. Abu Dhabi: Centre for Documentation and Research, 2007.

Majid, Ahmed. *Innovation Enhancement Mechanisms in the UAE.* [in Arabic]. Abu Dhabi: UAE Ministry of Economy, 2017.

Mohammad, Jassem. *Daesh, the Declaration of the Islamic State, and the Conflict over 'Al Bay'a'* [in Arabic]. Cairo: Al Maktab Al Arabi Lil Maaref, 2015.

Odeh, Jehad. *The Fall of the Brotherhood State* [in Arabic]. Cairo: Konooz Publishing and Distribution, 2013.

Park, Sangin. *Strategies and Policies in Digital Convergence.* Hershey: Idea Group Reference, 2007.

Ramadan, Zubeiri. *Globalization and the State's New Job Structure* [in Arabic]. Amman: Academic Book Center, 2015.

Rice, Mabrouk. *Repercussions of Financial Globalization on the Banking System* [in Arabic]. Amman: Dar Al Jenan Publishing and Distribution, 2016.

Salman, Jamal Dawood. *Knowledge Economy* [in Arabic]. Amman: Dar Al-Yazouri for Publishing and Distribution, 2012.

Shoaib, Hassib Abdel Halim. *A Teacher's Reference in the Teaching Methods of Arabic Language in the Primary, Middle, and Secondary School Levels* [in Arabic]. Beirut: Dar al-Kotob Al-Ilmlyah, 2015.

Smith, Anthony D. "Towards a Global Culture?" In *The Global Transformations Reader: An Introduction to the Globalization Debate,* edited by David Held and Anthony McGrew. Cambridge: Polity Press, 2000.

_____. *National Identity.* Las Vegas: University of Nevada Press, 1991.

Soros, George. *The Age of Fallibility: Consequences of the War on Terror.* New York Public Affairs, 2006.

Strange, Susan. *The Retreat of the State: The Diffusion of Power in the World Economy.* Cambridge: Cambridge University Press, 1996.

Talib, Talib Ghloum . *A Journey into the Affairs of Life* [in Arabic]. Giza: Atlas Publishing, 2016.

Yoshae, Ahmed Hesham. *The Globalization of Gulf Economy: Reading into the Bahraini Experience* [in Arabic]. Beirut: Arab Institute for Studies and Publishing, 2003.

Younis, Younis Muayad. *The Roles of the Great Asian Powers in the Strategic Balance in Asia after the Cold War and Their Future Prospects* [in Arabic]. Amman: Academic for Publishing & Distributing.

PERIODICALS

Abdel Salam, Rafik. "Arab elections: misplaced priorities" [in Arabic], *Democracy* (Cairo) August 31, 2018.

Al-Desouqi, Abu Baker. "Regional Organizations on a Crossroad," [in Arabic], *International Politics,* October 3, 2016.

Al-Saadi, Rashad Mohamed Salem. *The National Service and Its Security, Military, and Development Effects in the UAE* [in Arabic] (Abu Dhabi) 2015.

Arabi, Muslim Baba. "An Attempt to explore the concept of political reform" [in Arabic], *Cahiers de Politique & de Droit* no. 9, (Algiers: Université Kasdi Merbah Ouargla) June 2013.

Awfi, Mustafa, and Zainab Omrani. "National identity in light of modern information and communications technology" [in Arabic], *Ilum Al-Insan wa Al-Mujtamaa,* no. 4, (Algeria: University Mohamed Khider of Biskra) December 2012.

Awni, Malek. "Unified Challenge: Emerging regional power and trends in the evolution of the international leadership structure," [in Arabic], *International Politics,* October 14, 2014.

Bin Salem, Hasan Salem. "Daesh and Transborder Terrorism," [in Arabic], *Derasat Series,* no. 11 (Riyadh: King Faisal Center for Islamic Research and Studies, 2016).

Council for Scientific Research. "Toward the Knowledge Society," Issue 1: The Arab Knowledge Society and Its Role in Development" [in Arabic] (Riyadh: Scientific Research Council, King Abdulaziz University).

Dalah, Salem. "From the Rule of Law to Good Governance: Integration of Basis, Mechanisms, and Objective" [in Arabic], *Damascus University Journal for the Economic and Legal Sciences,* vol. 30, no. 2 (2014).

Elmawaldi, Awatef Outeil. "The Problem of Religious Extremism and the Cultural Identity of Society," [in Arabic], *Studies and Research Journal* no. 25 (Algiers, December 2016).

Hasan, Obaid Saleh. "Policies by UAE Legislator to Combating Cybercrimes" [in Arabic], *Al Fikr Al Sherati,* vol. 24, no. 95, (Sharjah, October 2015).

Hilal, Ali Al-Deen. "The State of the Arab Nation (2014-2015): The Hurricane...From Changing Regimes to Dissolving States" [in Arabic], *Arab Future Magazine*, no. 435 (Beirut, May 2015).

Ibrahim, Hassanein Tawfiq "The Obstacles of Democratic Transformation in Arab Spring Countries" [in Arabic], *Democracy* (Cairo) August 31, 2014

Izz-Al Din, Zeinab Hosni. "The Effect of 4GW on Arab National Security: ISIS as a Case Study," *International Politics* [in Arabic] (Cairo, August 10, 2017).

Karess, Heidi Issmat. "The Future of European Integration in Light of BREXIT," [in Arabic], *International Politics* website (Cairo, December 4, 2016).

Khalil, Sara. "Mathew Burrows' *Middle East 2020*: A Forward-looking View of the Region's Pathways" [in Arabic], *International Politics* (Cairo, October 15, 2014).

Marzouq, Rania. "The Geopolitical Implications of Low Oil Prices" [in Arabic], *International Politics* (Cairo), November 18, 2014.

Munser, Jamal. "The State in the Age of Globalization" [in Arabic], *Democracy Magazine*. Vol. 42 (Cairo, April, 2011).

Razak, Faten Mohammed, and Alaa Jabbar Ahmed. "The Weakness of the National Identity and Its Implication on the Iraqi National Security [in Arabic], *Asiyasiat wa Al-Duwalia* (Baghdad: University of Mustansiriyah, 2015).

"UAE National Service Law and promotion of identity" [in Arabic], *Nation Shield* (Abu Dhabi, 2014).

Younis, Mohammed Abdullah. "The Emirati Model: The Philosophy, Dimensions, and Indicators of Development in the UAE" [in Arabic], *Trending Events Journal of Attitudes* vol. 1, no. 5 (Abu Dhabi: Future for Advanced Research and Advanced Studies, December 2014).

Zaghouni, Rabeh. "Islamophobia and the Rise of the Extreme Right in Europe: A Socio-cultural Approach" [in Arabic], *Al Mustaqbal Al-Arabi*, no. 421 (Beirut: Centre for Arab Unity Studies, March, 2014).

DISSERTATIONS, CONFERENCE PAPERS, AND UNPUBLISHED STUDIES

Assiri, Abdul Rahman bin Mohammed. "Arab and International Experiences in Promoting the Values of Citizenship" [in Arabic]. Paper presented at the "Strengthening the Values of Citizenship and Its Role in Countering Terrorism" symposium. Naif Arab University for Security Sciences, Riyadh, November17-19, 2015.

Emirates Center for Strategic Studies and Research. "Position of the UAE citizens on the education system and the job market," unpublished poll. (Abu Dhabi, 2018).

_____. Project on Economic Diversification in the United Arab Emirates [in Arabic], Part 1, Executive Summary, unpublished study, (Abu Dhabi, 2001).

Khair, Arafah Mohammad Mohammad. "Weakness in Arabic in the Colleges of Education: Reasons, Effects, and Proposed Remedies" [in Arabic]. Paper presented at the Third Arabic Language Conference, Dubai, May 8-10, 2014.

Mousawi, Mohammad. "Investment in Human Capital and Its Effect on Economic Growth: Case of Algeria 1970-2011" [in Arabic]. PhD Diss., Faculty of Economic Sciences, Management and Commercial Sciences, University of Abou Bakr Belkaïd, Tlemcen (Algeria), 2015.

Salman, Ahed Taha Ayyal. "The Literature of Warfare of Imad ad-Din al-Isfahani" [in Arabic]. PhD Diss., Mu'tah University, Karak (Jordan), 2011.

NEWSPAPERS

Al Ahram (Cairo)

Al Arab (London)

Al Bayan (Dubai)

Al Eqtisadya (Riyadh)

Al Khaleej (Sharjah)

Al Sharq Al-Awsat (London)

Al-Ittihad (Abu Dhabi)

Al-Riyadh (Riyadh)

Emarat Alyoum (Dubai)

Gulf News (Abu Dhabi)

Hayat (London)

Khaleej Times (Sharjah)

The National (Abu Dhabi)

WEBSITES

Akhbarak. http://www.akhbarak.net

Al Ain News. https://www.government.ae

Al Kashif Center. http://alkashif.org

Al Mezmaah Studies and Research Center. http://www.almezmaah.com

Algerian Encyclopedia for Political and Strategic Studies. https://www.politics-dz.com

Almanhal. https://www.almanhal.com

Arab Center for Research and Studies. http://www.acrseg.org

Arab Scientific Center for Research and Humanities Studies. http://arab-csr.org

Bahraini Ministry of Interior. https://www.policemc.gov.bh

Carnegie Endowment. http://carnegieendowment.org

CNN. https://arabic.cnn.com

Democratic Arab Center for Strategic, Political, and Economic Studies. http://democraticac.de

Elaph. http://elaph.com

Emirates Center for Strategic Studies and Research. http://www.ecssr.ac.ae

Emirates News Agency. wam.ae

Faselah. http://faselah.net

Future Center for Advanced Research and Studies. https://futureuae.com

Global Future Councils. https://www.weforum.org/communities/global-future-councils

Hassiba Benbouali University of Chlef. http://www.univ-chlef.dz

Middle East Online. http://middle-east-online.com

Mominoun Without Borders. http://www.mominoun.com

Official Portal of the UAE Government. https://www.government.ae

Reuters. https://reuters.com

Shamela Library. http://shamela.ws

Strategic Fiker Center for Studies. http://fikercenter.com

The National Qualifications Authority. https://www.nqa.gov.ae

Transparency International. http://www.transparency.org

UAE Cabinet. https://www.uaecabinet.ae

UAE Centennial 2071. https://area2071.ae

UAE Judicial Department. https://www.adjd.gov.ae

UAE Ministry of Cabinet Affairs and the Future. https://www.mocaf.gov.ae

UAE Ministry of Economy. www.economy.gov.ae

UAE Ministry of Education. https://www.moe.gov.ae

UAE Ministry of State for Federal National Council Affairs. www.mfnca.gov.ae

UAE Platform for Future Foresight. https://uaefutureforesight.ae

UAE Space Agency. http://www.space.gov.ae

UAE Strategy for Artificial Intelligence (AI). http://www.uaeai.ae/en/

UAE Vision 2021. https://www.vision2021.ae

UNESCO. https://ar.unesco.org

United Nations. https://www.un.org/ar/index.html

Watani Al Emarat Foundation. http://watani-alemarat.ae

World Bank. https://blogs.worldbank.org

World Bank. https://data.albankaldawli.org

ARTICLES AND REPORTS

Bogost, Ian. "Apple Is Worth One Trillion Dollars." *The Atlantic.* August 2, 2018. https://bit.ly/2OEENKo.

BP. "BP Statistical Review of World Energy." June 2016. https://on.bp.com/2bSW4Mf.

BP. "BP Statistical Review of World Energy." June 2017. https://on.bp.com/2IIOAeS.

Butti, Maryam, Ilke Denizli, and Tarik Chelali, "The Martyr and the Nation: The UAE, Turkey, and Algeria," Delma Institute, May 22, 2018, http://drafts.delma.io/en/the-martyr-and-the-nation-the-uae-turkey-and-algeria.

CIA World Fact Book. "United Arab Emirates." Last modified May 1, 2018. https://www.cia.gov/library/publications/the-world-factbook/geos/ae.html.

Clinton, Hillary Rodham. "Leading Through Civilian Power: Redefining American Diplomacy and Development." *Foreign Affairs*, October 1, 2010. https://fam.ag/2GPWJl9.

Coker, Margaret, Eric Schmitt, and Rukmini Callimachi. "With Loss of Its Caliphate, ISIS May Return to Guerrilla Roots." *New York Times*, October 18, 2017.

El-Erian, Mohamed A. "This Era of Low-Cost Oil Is Different." *Bloomberg*, December 29, 2014. https://www.bloomberg.com/view/articles/2014-12-29/this-era-of-lowcost-oil-is-different.

Elmasry, Tarek, Enrico Benni, Jigar Patel, Jan Peter and Dem Moore. "Digital Middle East: Transforming the region into a leading digital economy." McKinsey. Last modified October 2016. https://bit.ly/2EJRgHA.

Europol. "Serious and Organized Crime… Threat Assessment, Crime in The Age of Technology." Last modified March 2017. https://bit.ly/2na2zQR.

Georgetown Institute for Women, Peace and Security and Peace Research Institute Oslo. *Women, Peace and Security Index 2017/18: Tracking*

Sustainable Peace through Inclusion, Justice, and Security for Women. Washington, DC: GIWPS and PRIO, 2017. https://bit.ly/2j2egIY.

Grayling, A. C. "Prepare for the post-oil era." *The Guardian*, March 14, 2007.

Halliday, Fred. "Globalization: good or bad?" LSE Roundtable Discussion. October 2000.

Helliwell, John, Richard Layard, and Jeffrey Sachs, eds. *World Happiness Report 2017.* New York: Sustainable Development Solutions Network, 2017. http://worldhappiness.report/ed/2017/.

IMD World Competitiveness Center. "IMD World Digital Competitiveness Ranking 2017." Last modified 2017. https://www.imd.org/globalassets/wcc/docs/release-2017/2017-world_competitiveness_ranking.pdf.

IMD World Competitiveness Center. "IMD World Talent Report 2016." Last modified November 2016. https://www.imd.org/globalassets/wcc/docs/talent_2016_ web.pdf.

Internet World Stats. "Internet Growth Statistics 1995 to 2017 - the Global Village Online." Last modified April 16, 2018. https://www.internetworldstats.com/emarketing.htm.

James, Lewis. "Economic Impact of Cybercrime—No Slowing Down." McAfee. Last modified February 2018. https://bit.ly/2EMuUtb.

Lange, Glenn-Marie, Quentin Wodon, and Kevin Carey eds. *The Changing Wealth of Nations 2018: Building a Sustainable Future.* Washington, DC: International Bank for Reconstruction and Development / The World Bank, 2018. https://bit.ly/2EnkWdu.

"Oil and the Alternative Energy Resources" [in Arabic]. *Akhbar Al Saah* vol. 7, no. 2075. (Abu Dhabi), January 23, 2002.

Rubin, Michael. "The age of hyper-terrorism and 'low cost' terrorism." *The American Enterprise Institute*, February 10, 2017. http://www.aei.org/publication/the-age-of-hyper-terrorism-and-low-cost-terrorism/.

Stoller, Kristin. "The World's Largest Tech Companies 2017: Apple and Samsung Lead, Facebook Rises." *Forbes*, May 24, 2017. https://bit.ly/2GRs5UB.

Transparency International. "Corruption Perceptions Index 2017." Last modified February 21, 2018. https://www.transparency.org/news/feature/corruption_perceptions_index_2017.

The Institute for Energy Research (IER). "New Oil Finds Around the Globe: Will the U.S. Capitalize on Its Oil Resources?" Last modified September 13, 2011. http://instituteforenergyresearch.org/studies/new-oil-finds-around-the-globe-will-the-u-s-capitalize-on-its-oil-resources/.

The White House. "National Security Strategy of the United States of America." December 2017. https://bit.ly/2CzLLd7.

The World Justice Project. *Rule of Law Index, 2017–2018*. Washington, DC: The World Justice Project, 2018. https://worldjusticeproject.org/sites/default/files/documents/WJP_ROLI_2017-18_Online-Edition.pdf.

UAE Gender Balance Council. *Gender Balance Guide*. Paris: OECD Publishing, 2017. https://www.oecd.org/gov/gender-balance-guide-uae-2017.pdf.

"UAE: Pioneers Initiatives Based on Future Technology" [in Arabic]. *Akhbar Al Saah* vol. 24, no. 6451. (Abu Dhabi) September 24, 2017.

United Nations Development Programme. *Human Development Report 2002*. New York: Oxford University Press, 2002. http://hdr.undp.org/sites/default/files/reports/263/hdr_2002_en_complete.pdf.

United States International Trade Commission. "Global Digital Trade 1: Market Opportunities and Key Foreign Trade Restrictions." USITC Publication 4716. August 2017. https://www.usitc.gov/publications/332/pub4716.pdf.

Wilkinson, Tracy. "Trump's 'America first' policy changes U.S. role on global stage." *Los Angeles Times*, June 2, 2017.

World Economic Forum. *The Global Gender Gap Report 2017*. Geneva: World Economic Forum, 2017. http://www3.weforum.org/docs/WEF_GGGR_2017.pdf.

World Economic Forum. *The Global Human Capital Report 2017*. Geneva: World Economic Forum, 2017. https://weforum.ent.box.com/s/dari4dktg4jt2g9xo2o5pksjpatvawdb.

Zogby, James. "Muslim Millennials' Views on Religion," Huff Post. January 9, 2016. https://bit.ly/2oish7F.

"The generation of the present is the generation of the future; thus, there needs to be inter-generational solidarity. The old generation has a duty to be a role model for the youth; and a role model embodies good ethics and hard work."

Zayed bin Sultan Al Nahyan